NEB

TWENTIETH-CENTURY WOMEN POLITICIANS

TWENTIETH-CENTURY WOMEN POLITICIANS

ELLEN THRO

Facts On File, Inc.

American Profiles: Twentieth-Century Women Politicians

Facts On File, Inc.
11 Penn Plaza
New York, NY 10001

Library of Congress Cataloging-in-Publication Data

Thro, Ellen.
    Twentieth-century women politicians / Ellen Thro.
        p. cm. — (American profiles)
    Includes bibliographical references and index.
    Summary: Brief biographies of ten women influential in modern
American politics: Margaret Chase Smith, Nancy Kassebaum, Dianne
Feinstein, Ann Richards, Geraldine Ferraro, Maxine Waters, Patricia
Schroeder, Christine Todd Whitman, Carol Moseley-Braun, and Ileana
Ros-Lehtinen.
    ISBN 0-8160-3758-2
    1. Women in politics—United States—Biography—Juvenile
literature. 2. Women   legislators—United States—Biography—
Juvenile literature. 3. Women governors—United States—Biography—
Juvenile literature. 4. Governors. [1. Women legislators.
2. Women governors. 3. Legislators. 4. Women in politics.
5. Women—Biography.] I. Title. II. Series: American profiles
(Facts on File, Inc.)
HQ1236.5.U6T76   1998
305.43′329′092273—dc21   ▼ 97-51878

Text design by Cathy Rincon
Cover design by Matt Galemmo

Printed in the United States of America.

MP FOF 10 9 8 7 6 5 4 3 2 1

This book is printed on acid-free paper.

Contents

Acknowledgments

M y thanks to Senator Dianne Feinstein, Senator Carol Moseley-Braun, Representative Ileana Ros-Lehtinen, and Governor Christine Todd Whitman. Thanks also to my editors, Nicole Bowen and Terence Maikels, and the Facts On File production staff.

Introduction

Who are "women politicians"?

Some are youthful; others are mature. Some have long-lasting marriages; others are widowed, divorced, or remarried. Some were born into working class families; others grew up in inner city housing projects. Some come from political families. Some were born in a foreign country and are naturalized Americans. Many are mothers and grandmothers.

They are women who chose to be politicians, weighing that career against other professions and often against the importance of husbands and children. Before entering elective office, some practiced law; others were teachers or business owners. A few stayed at home with their children.

In other words, "women politicians" are women like most people's mothers and grandmothers. They're no different from the woman any girl might become.

Women politicians are also very much like men politicians. They love the challenge of the campaign, the political maneuvering, and the public recognition. Until recently, the main difference was that women had to campaign against the doubts of both men and women that they had "the right stuff" to be successful in politics—the boldness to stand up under pressure and the courage to succeed. Unlike men, women were often asked whether they could handle both a political career and a family. Fortunately, those doubts have almost entirely disappeared.

The 10 women in this book are pioneers. The election of each one marked a "first" in the governor's office, or in Congress, or in nomination for the nation's second-highest office. Happily, there were many successful women from whom to choose. These 10 were selected to represent the different regions of the country, both major political parties, and a variety of racial and ethnic groups.

Margaret Chase Smith (Maine) was a middle-aged widow when she began her congressional career. Patricia Schroeder (Colorado) began her House career as a young mother, toilet training her toddlers in her office and giving birthday parties for five-year-olds in the House members' dining room.

Ann Richards (Texas) stopped being a full-time housewife and mother to enter politics, knowing that her choice might play a role in destroying her marriage. It did.

These 10 women took different political routes to national or state-wide office. In her first electoral campaign, Geraldine Ferraro (New York) won a seat in Congress. Six years later, her party nominated her for vice president. Dianne Feinstein (California) was a longtime county supervisor and big city mayor, and an unsuccessful candidate for governor, before winning an election for the U.S. Senate.

Carol Moseley-Braun (Illinois) and Maxine Waters (California) both had successful careers in their state legislatures before entering Congress. Ileana Ros-Lehtinen (Florida), a naturalized American, was the owner of a private bilingual school before running successfully for the Florida legislature and then the U.S. House of Representatives.

Nancy L. Kassebaum (Kansas) served only on a local school board before successfully running for the Senate. Christine Todd Whitman (New Jersey) held a position in the governor's cabinet before winning her first statewide election to become governor. Both women came from prominent political families.

The political opportunities of these 10 women have their origins in the efforts of generations of women suffragists—the women who campaigned from the 19th into the 20th century until the 19th Amendment to the Constitution gave them the right to vote in 1920.

A few states allowed women to vote before this amendment was passed: Wyoming allowed it starting in 1869 and Montana in 1914, for instance. A Montanan, Jeannette Rankin, was the first woman elected to the U.S. House of Representatives, in 1916. Nellie Tayloe Ross from Wyoming and Miriam A. Ferguson from Texas were the first women elected state governors, in 1925. Hattie Wyatt Caraway of Arkansas was the first woman elected as U.S. Senator, in 1932.

Even in the 1990s, political "firsts" are being recorded. Not until 1992 did a state (California) elect two women to the Senate at the same time. Not until 1996 did a woman senator (Nancy Kassebaum) chair an important committee.

Other "firsts" are still waiting to be tallied. No woman has been nominated for president—yet. Both the House of Representatives and the Senate will need many more women before they reach 50 percent of the membership. Right now, it's below 10 percent, but higher than the 1–2 percent in the 1980s. The number of women governors is equally small.

Many state legislatures have higher percentages of women than the U.S. Congress has. Almost 50 percent of Washington state senators, for instance, are women. Each state and local area also have "firsts"—the first state representative and senator, the first woman mayor, the first woman county supervisor. Perhaps before the end of the century, some or all of these "firsts" will have been accomplished.

Margaret Chase Smith

(1897–1995)

The year was 1950. The United States was caught in the grip of an anti-Communist hysteria that became known as McCarthyism —named after the man who led the movement, Senator Joseph McCarthy of Wisconsin. Many people, including most senators, were afraid to speak out against McCarthy's extremism for fear that they themselves would be branded "Communists." Every senator was silent, except for one of McCarthy's fellow Republicans—Senator Margaret Chase Smith of Maine, then the only woman senator. Although Smith rarely made speeches, as a matter of conscience she could not remain quiet. In a 30-year political career based on principle and independent spirit, this was perhaps her finest hour.

Margaret Madeline Chase was born on December 14, 1897, in the small Maine city of Skowhegan. She was the oldest of six children. Her father, George Chase, a barber and a waiter, came from a family long-settled in New England. Her mother, Carrie

Senator Margaret Chase Smith at her desk in Washington in 1949, wearing her signature fresh rose (AP/Wide World Photos)

Murray Chase, had a New England–settler mother and a French-Canadian father. Murray worked in a shoe factory before marrying and took part-time jobs later.

Margaret Chase began working when she was 13, taking various sales and waitressing jobs after school and on weekends. She was an average student, more interested in basketball than in scholarship. She took a commercial course at Skowhegan High School, learning office skills such as shorthand and bookkeeping. Despite her 5-foot-3-inch height, she was a star of the women's basketball team, which won the state championship in her senior year. She was also the team manager.

While working as a night telephone operator she became friendly with many people in town, including a 40-year-old politician named Clyde Smith. As first selectman, he was the town's chief elected official. He recommended her for her first full-time job, in the town's tax assessment office; she was still in high school. Margaret graduated from high school in 1916.

Her dream was to go to college and become a physical education teacher, but the Chases were too poor to pay for college. After a short-lived job teaching in a nearby rural one-room school, she took a series of office jobs in Skowhegan with the telephone company, the local weekly newspaper, and a woolen mill. In 1918 and 1919, she also helped coach the high school basketball team to winning seasons.

In 1920, the 19th Amendment to the U.S. Constitution, which guaranteed women the right to vote, was passed. Margaret Chase, like many women, examined her newly expanded rights and became active in several women's organizations. She was especially active in the local Business and Professional Women's Club, which was open to any woman with a job and was not linked to any political organization. In 1923 and 1924 she was elected to consecutive one-year terms as its president. In 1926, she was elected president of the Maine Federation of Business and Professional Women's Clubs. She was elected as a delegate to the local Republican District Committee in 1928.

Margaret had various boyfriends in high school and during her twenties, but her most lasting relationship was with Clyde Smith, a progressive Republican. The two were married on May 14, 1930. As was customary, she quit her job to become a full-time wife and to assist Clyde with his political campaigns.

When Clyde Smith was elected to the U.S. House of Representatives in 1936, she happily joined social organizations for the wives of congressmen and other high officials. However, she also stepped beyond the conventional political wife's role. Many women unofficially helped in their husbands' offices and campaigns, but Margaret convinced Clyde to list her on his payroll as his secretary.

In 1940, shortly before the Maine primary election, Clyde suffered a serious heart attack. Margaret and Clyde decided that she would run for election. If Clyde recovered, she would step aside and he would resume his race. But Clyde died. At first, Maine Republican leaders assumed that they could support Margaret's candidacy for the few months of Clyde's unexpired term as a mark of respect for him. That obligation fulfilled, a "real" candidate would run for the next full term. Smith, though, ran for both the unexpired term and the full term in elections held within a three-month period. She won both of them.

Some women had already served multiple terms in the U.S. House when Margaret was first elected. But Smith's deliberately cultivated "ladylike" style and her intentionally high profile caught the attention of a wider audience than usual. She began to wear a fresh rose each day in a little container of water that was pinned to her lapel like a corsage. The rose became her political and personal trademark. Later a rose grower developed a special variety and in her honor named it the Margaret Chase Smith.

By 1948, Smith had been elected senator from Maine. Her behavior on the House and Senate floors revealed a plain-spoken woman who made decisions based on her own convictions. Never acting merely to please her constituents or party leaders, she was a moderate in an increasingly conservative party, but strong support in her home district assured her numerous reelections to both houses of Congress. In her 1950 "Declaration of Conscience" speech, she denounced the extremism of the Far Right (conservative anti-Communists). On the

Smith, campaigning for president in 1964, laughs when she spots a rival's campaign button on a prospective voter. (AP/World Wide Photos)

Smith campaigns in New Hampshire for the Republican presidential nomination with Dartmouth College students in 1964. (AP/World Wide Photos)

20th anniversary of the speech, in 1970, she spoke out against the extremism of the Far Left.

Although she always said she was not a "feminist," Smith supported Equal Rights Amendment bills throughout the 1940s. Also, she worked to improve the status of women in the military services. During World War II, she joined other women Representatives to restore funds to provide daycare for children of women who worked in military supply factories.

Her vote-getting abilities among Maine voters encouraged the Democrats to run a woman candidate, Lucia Cormier, against her in 1960. Cormier was the Democratic floor leader in the state legislature. In the first major election in U.S. history between two women nominated by major parties, Smith won easily.

Smith's independence delighted Maine voters, and in the early 1950s, Republicans began speaking of her as a possible nominee for vice president or even for president. But her voting record and her moderate beliefs greatly reduced her chances for nomination to either post. Though she ran for the Republican presidential nomination in 1964, she had no real chance of winning. The Republican party by then was firmly in the hands of extreme conservatives, and Senator Barry Goldwater was nominated.

Smith's record of service to her country rests on four major issues that are still important today. First, she sought to improve the status of women serving in the armed forces during World War II. The first major bill she introduced in the House, in 1943, was to allow the women's branch of the navy—the WAVES (Women Accepted for Voluntary Emergency Service)—to serve worldwide, as army women did. The bill passed but was modified to let women serve only in the Western Hemisphere.

In 1947, with a Republican majority in the House, she became chairwoman of the House of Representatives' Armed Services Committee's subcommittee on Hospitalization and Medicine. One of the first bills Smith supported was one that would make army and navy nurses regular and permanent members of the service with full pay and benefits. At one point, she learned that another armed services subcommittee had put the proposal on hold after off-the-record, closed-door sessions with navy representatives. Angered, she accused the military of dodging the issue. Single-handedly, she forced the issue to votes in her committee and (through a parliamentary maneuver) on the House floor, where it lost both times. She didn't give up. Finally, after asking for help from the secretary of defense, the bill passed. In 1948, President Harry Truman signed it into law.

The second major issue Smith fought for was unification of the armed forces, following World War II. Smith, already a supporter of a unified military

> **M**y creed
> *[for public service] is
> . . . that constructive
> criticism is not only
> to be expected but
> sought, that smears
> are not only to
> be expected but
> fought, that honor is
> to be earned but
> not bought.*
>
> —Margaret Chase Smith

with a separate air force, joined the Naval Affairs Committee in 1943. In 1947, she helped pass a law that created the air force and that also allowed the joint chiefs of staff to govern all the military services. For her work, she was commissioned a lieutenant-colonel in the Air Force Reserve.

Third was Smith's leadership in denouncing McCarthyism in the early 1950s. The cold war between the United States and the Communist-ruled Soviet Union (including modern Russia) had begun in the late 1940s. By 1948, the Soviet Union or Soviet-controlled puppet regimes took control of eastern Europe. The Soviet Union developed an atomic bomb in 1949, and by 1950 China was also ruled by Communists. The Korean Conflict had just begun over an invasion of U.S.-supported Korea by Communist-supported North Korea.

> I *don't want to see the Republican Party ride to political victory on the Four Horsemen of Calumny—Fear, Ignorance, Bigotry, and Smear.*
>
> —Margaret Chase Smith

Senator Joseph McCarthy of Wisconsin and other Communist-hunters, such as Richard M. Nixon, representative (and later senator) from California, seemed to answer the needs of many Americans frightened by Communist victories abroad. These politicians' extremism led many Americans to believe that the nation was also threatened by Communists who had already infiltrated the government and popular entertainment industries. If this were true, they believed that Communism was also corrupting American freedoms and values from within.

McCarthy first came to national attention in February 1950, when he claimed that the U.S. State Department was heavily infiltrated by Communist party members. Smith was initially drawn to McCarthy's charges, but she reserved final judgment until he produced proof—something he never did to her satisfaction.

As she said later, she began to wonder about the validity, accuracy, credibility, and fairness of his charges: McCarthy labeled anyone who disagreed with him or questioned his methods a Communist. His charisma made him powerful. In the climate of postwar America, the fear of Communism was widespread and McCarthy made the most of his charges on the Senate floor, where—unlike a court of law—he didn't have to prove any of them. Also, his senatorial immunity protected him from being sued.

Communist-hunting was also going on in the House of Representatives, principally by the House Un-American Activities Committee (HUAC). One of the most prominent committee members was Representative Nixon, who had won his first congressional electoral campaign by questioning the patriotism of his opponent.

HUAC held a series of hearings at which many people suspected of being Communists or Communist sympathizers were called to testify about their political activities or beliefs. They were also encouraged to name others as Communists or sympathizers (called "fellow travelers").

> T*he American people are sick and tired of being afraid to speak their minds lest they be politically smeared as communists or fascists. . . . They're sick and tired of seeing innocent people smeared and guilty people whitewashed.*
>
> —Margaret Chase Smith

Unlike a court, a committee hearing didn't allow accused people the right to present a defense. Those who refused to testify were cited for contempt of Congress and some were jailed. In addition, the movie and entertainment industry and others had "blacklists" containing the names of such "Communists," preventing them from being hired.

McCarthyism in the Senate was an escalation of this climate of fear. When Smith, then a first-term senator, realized that no other senator was going to take McCarthy on, she felt that it was up to her.

In her "Declaration of Conscience" speech, Smith spoke about the way character assassination was lowering the moral quality of American government and asked the Senate to think carefully about the use and abuse of power. At the end of her speech she listed the names of seven Republican senators who agreed with her.

Public reaction and editorial reaction from the press strongly supported her. But McCarthy punished her politically by removing her from an investigating subcommittee, replacing her with Nixon, who had just been elected to the Senate. The Senate leadership also removed her from the Senate Republican Committee.

The fourth major issue in Smith's political career was the close questioning of the language of the Partial Test Ban Treaty, in 1963, and its effect on the United States's ability to detect foreign nuclear tests and protect the country's own nuclear strike capability. In this treaty, the United States, the Soviet Union, and the United Kingdom agreed not to perform any nuclear testing where radioactive fallout would spread outside the country conducting the test.

Smith felt that not enough had been said about the treaty's disadvantages. When the administration couldn't answer her specific questions about it, she reluctantly voted "No."

The treaty was ratified, 80 to 19. Smith's "No" vote was used against her in her 1966 reelection campaign as a sign that she was against peace. But the questions she raised led to the establishment of the Subcommittee on Safeguards on the Test Ban Treaty, an attempt to assure Soviet compliance with it. Smith was appointed to the subcommittee.

Since her first election to the House in 1940 and first election to the Senate in 1948, Smith had been immensely popular with Maine voters and was never defeated at the polls. By the end of the 1960s, however, Smith seemed to have lost touch with her voting public. The Democratic party grew in strength in Maine. While her 1950 "Declaration of Conscience" speech had been considered cutting edge her 1970 update sounded behind the times. Another speech, which warned women that the freedom gained by the birth control pill needed to be accompanied by responsibility, sounded preachy to many. In 1972, running for her fifth Senate term, she was defeated and retired to her hometown. Margaret Chase Smith died in Skowhegan on May 29, 1995, at the age of 97.

In her career, Smith was the first woman to be elected to the Senate without having first been appointed to serve the remainder of someone else's term. She was also the first woman to be elected to both the House of Representatives and the Senate. And she was the first woman to defend her position against another woman in a major election.

Chronology

DECEMBER 14, 1897	Margaret Madeline Chase is born in Skowhegan, Maine
1916	graduates from Skowhegan High School
1922	founds Skowhegan chapter of the Business and Professional Women's Club
1923–24	serves as president of Skowhegan's Business and Professional Women's Club
1926	is elected president of the Maine Federation of Business and Professional Women's Clubs
1928	is elected as a delegate to her local Republican District Committee
1930	marries Clyde Smith, a member of the Maine legislature; is named Republican state committeewoman from her county
1935	is named a member of the Republican State Committee
1940	Clyde Smith dies; Margaret Smith wins a special election to fill out Clyde's unexpired term and the general election for a full term in the U.S. House of Representatives
1942, 1944, 1946	is reelected to the U.S. House of Representatives
1943	The WAVES (Women Accepted for Voluntary Emergency Service) bill is passed; Smith is nicknamed "Mother of the WAVES"
1947	is commissioned as a lieutenant-colonel in the U.S. Air Force Reserve

1948	is elected to the U.S. Senate
1949	is voted "Woman of the Year" by the Associated Press
1950	delivers "Declaration of Conscience" speech denouncing McCarthyism
1954, 1960, 1966	is reelected to the U.S. Senate
1964	announces candidacy for Republican nomination for president; is defeated by Sen. Barry Goldwater
1970	updates her "Declaration of Conscience" Speech on its 20th anniversary
1972	is defeated for reelection to the U.S. Senate
MAY 29, 1995	Margaret Chase Smith dies in Skowhegan

Further Reading

Fleming, Alice (Mulcahey). *The Senator from Maine: Margaret Chase Smith.* New York: Crowell, 1969. A young people's biography, written at a time when a woman politician was a novelty. Now out of print but may still be in libraries.

Graham, Frank. *Margaret Chase Smith: Woman of Courage.* New York: John Day, 1964. A biography that emphasizes Smith as a celebrity as much as a legislator, at a time when a woman politician was a rarity.

Pollack, Jill S. *Women on the Hill: A History of Women in Congress.* Danbury, Conn.: Franklin Watts, 1996.

Schmidt, Patricia L. *Margaret Chase Smith: Beyond Convention.* Orono, Maine: University of Maine Press, 1997. This biography contains much information not found in others, but it also contains some errors about well-known facts.

Smith, Margaret Chase. *Declaration of Conscience.* Edited by William C. Lewis, Jr. New York: Doubleday & Company, 1972. Original text of many of her most important bills. Lewis, her longtime chief of staff and close friend, provides context about the politics and people involved. Out of print but still available in some libraries.

Wallace, Patricia Ward. *Politics of Conscience: A Biography of Margaret Chase Smith*. Westport, Conn.: Praeger, 1995. A solid, illustrated biography.

Nancy L. Kassebaum

(1932–)

For 20 years, Nancy L. Kassebaum had been a homemaker and the mother of four children. She had also served on the local school board and on statewide committees supporting the humanities and governmental ethics. Now her marriage was ending. She needed to lead her life in a new direction. She accepted a job in the Washington office of a Kansas senator. Three years later, the senator announced his retirement. Kassebaum decided to run for the vacant seat. After all, her middle initial stood for Landon—a name that Kansans knew and trusted. Now was her chance to make her own political career, an idea she had considered before getting married.

She campaigned and won the election, becoming the first woman to be elected senator without having ever served before in Congress.

Nancy Landon, the daughter of political figure Alfred M. ("Alf") Landon and his second wife, Theo Cobb Landon, was born on July 29, 1932. She was third in line, after a half-sister and a brother. Soon after her birth, in 1932, her father was elected to the first of two terms

Senator Nancy L. Kassebaum announces she will not run for reelection in 1996.
(AP/World Wide Photos)

as governor of Kansas. In 1936, he ran unsuccessfully as the Republican presidential candidate. Despite this setback, Landon continued
to be a force in Kansas politics, since Kansas remained a largely

Republican state. He became known as "the grand old man of the Grand Old Party" (a Republican nickname).

Though the governor's mansion was her early childhood home, Kassebaum today doesn't remember those years. Instead she remembers Alf Landon's political role after he retired from electoral office. A stream of political figures visited the family home, and she lay in bed at night listening to political conversations through an air vent in the floor.

After graduating from high school in Topeka, Nancy Landon earned a bachelor's degree in political science from the University of Kansas in 1954 and a master's in diplomatic history from the University of Minnesota in 1956. She had the training and the family background for a political career, but in those days it seemed more like a fantasy than a possibility.

In 1956, she married Philip Kassebaum, a friend from the University of Kansas. The couple moved to a farm near the small town of Maize, in the Wichita area. Philip pursued a career as a lawyer and businessman. Typical of the 1950s and 1960s, Nancy was a housewife and eventually became the mother of four children: Philip Jr., Linda, Richard, and William. Outside the home, she served on a statewide commission on governmental ethics and on a committee supporting the humanities. She was also an officer in a family company that owned several radio stations. The closest she came, though, to electoral politics was winning a seat on her local school board.

Then, in 1975, her life changed; she obtained a legal separation from her husband. They would divorce in 1979. James Pearson, one of Kansas's senators, offered her a job in his Washington office, assisting Kansans who were dealing with federal agencies. This new direction was what her life needed. She took the job.

In 1978, she was given a second opportunity in the political world. Pearson decided to retire from office. Kassebaum considered running for statewide office on the Republican

> I believed I could contribute something . . . But I would not have [run] if I had not thought I had a . . . chance of winning.
>
> —Nancy L. Kassebaum

> I*t has been said
> I am riding on the
> coattails of my dad.
> But I can't think
> of any better
> coattails to ride on.*
>
> —Nancy L. Kassebaum

ticket. As an educated woman and a politician's daughter, she saw both the opportunities for service and the practical side of a political campaign.

Alf Landon wasn't so sure Kansas was ready for a woman senator and wasn't sure his daughter was up to a statewide campaign. But her mother encouraged her. So did her former husband, telling her that if she had a "gnawing in her stomach" to run, she could handle the campaign.

Kassebaum defeated seven other candidates in the primary, capturing 31 percent of the vote. In the general election, she ran as a fresh face and openly admitted to riding on her father's coattails.

Despite charges that she didn't pay her fair share of income taxes, she refused to make public the joint tax return she filed with her former husband. She lost ground in public opinion polls on this issue. But on election day, she defeated, with 56 percent of the vote, Democrat Bill Roy (who had narrowly lost the last senatorial election to Senator Bob Dole).

Nationally, there was skepticism about her election. One newspaper noted that if her middle name had been Jones, her campaign would have been a joke. And, in a time when a woman legislator was often viewed with condescension by male colleagues, she had the disadvantage of being the only woman in the Senate. She avoided being labeled a feminist, preferring the term "humanist," and she handled some of the gender problems with humor, rather than with anger.

She did recognize that some male senators didn't think she could handle "men's issues" like defense spending and legislative maneuvering. So, she quietly studied the issues and worked her way through the senatorial hierarchy to accomplish her legislative goals. She was appointed to the Banking, Housing and Urban Affairs, Budget, Commerce, and Science and Transportation committees and the Special Committee on Aging. When the opportunity came, she traded her Banking Committee seat for one on the Foreign Relations Committee. She later achieved her greatest power on the Labor and Human Resources Committee.

Kassebaum was a Republican from a conservative state, and her voting record reflected that in her early days in the Senate. She favored a balanced budget but thought there was little chance of having one soon. She opposed President Jimmy Carter's embargo of grain shipments to the Soviet Union, believing it would mainly harm American farmers, such as those in Kansas. Always a fiscal conservative, she supported President Ronald Reagan's cuts in federal spending and tax rates during the 1980s.

With foreign policy legislation, she was more liberal. Even though many Kansans opposed it, she supported a treaty to give control of the Panama Canal to Panama. She favored the Strategic Arms Limitation Treaty (SALT), which cut the number of nuclear weapons worldwide. She also supported full diplomatic relations with China. She opposed a controversial effort to supply aid to rebels in the African nation of Angola, however, fearing it would harm U.S. relations with other African nations.

She was also more liberal on issues important to women. She urged President Reagan (unsuccessfully) to include the Equal Rights Amendment as part of the Republican platform. She supported federal funding of abortions in cases where the mother's life was in danger or when the pregnancy resulted from rape or incest.

After reelection to the Senate in 1984 and in 1990, she gained seniority, yet she never strayed far from the Republican leadership's position on issues. Instead she carved out a balance between them and her own individual positions, and she formed partnerships with Democrats on issues that she considered important to the nation.

Her ability to gain the maximum value from the senatorial system was best seen in her final years in office. This was a time when extreme conservatives had gained control of the Republican party. In 1994, they won a majority in both houses of Congress for the first time in 30 years.

The Republican agenda had three major points: to create a balanced budget, to reduce taxes, and to reduce the scope of federal programs in people's lives. Kassebaum became chairwoman of the Senate Labor and Human Resources Committee, the first time a woman headed a major Senate committee. She agreed with the Republican priorities, but she worried that if carried too far, they would remove the safety net that protected the poor, the disabled, and other vulnerable citizens.

She put her own stamp on Republican legislation in three ways: as Labor and Human Resources Committee chair and as an important member of other committees; as part of a small group of moderate Republicans who wanted to preserve health, welfare, education, and foreign aid programs; and as a partner with Democrats to produce nonpartisan legislation on selected issues.

As committee chairwoman, Kassebaum introduced a job-training bill that replaced highly specific federal programs with block grants to the states—money that states could use in programs that met their own citizens' needs. She called it reforming job training by wiping the slate clean. She sponsored a bill that reduced spending, but retained funding for community-based public health programs, including minority recruiting.

She also convinced the conservative chairman of the Foreign Relations Committee to drop proposals that restricted funding for United Nations (U.N.) peacekeeping operations. The committee also adopted her proposal to transfer antidrug funds to economic assistance programs for underdeveloped nations. She later worked with Senator Dianne Feinstein, a Democrat from California, to authorize money for an Asian Development Bank.

Kassebaum was the chief sponsor of a bill to make the student-loan program more efficient and less costly. The National Endowments for the Arts and the Humanities were also high-priority items for her at a time when some Republicans wanted to eliminate them from the budget. They are part of Americans' national heritage, she insisted.

She was one of a core group of six moderate Republicans who often proposed legislation and voted as a bloc on selected legislation. Since the Senate's Republicans held a majority just by three people, the moderates were able to influence legislation in committees and on the Senate floor. Their strategy: If they voted against a bill, it might lose; if it reflected their values, their votes would make sure it passed.

As part of the moderate group, Kassebaum sponsored a bill to prevent states from transferring child care funds to welfare programs. She restored almost $6 billion to the subsidy program for college loans. She also helped retain funding for Medicaid (the most important medical program for poor people) that the Republican leadership wanted to remove.

Some of the most important legislation Kassebaum introduced was written with Democrats, chiefly Senator Edward Kennedy from

Kassebaum, chair of the Senate Labor and Human Resources Committee, and Senator Edward Kennedy (right) of Massachusetts, ranking Democratic member, introduce a candidate for surgeon general before his confirmation hearings in 1995. (AP/World Wide Photos)

Massachusetts, the former chairman of the Labor and Human Resources Committee. Their bill supporting treatment of AIDS gave more money and control to individual states, while reducing overall spending. It also required states to adopt guidelines for the counselling of HIV-positive patients and for voluntary HIV testing of pregnant women.

Their legislation also provided funds for child care for low-income families. Kassebaum said it balanced reduced federal regulation with recognition of the government's role in making child care available to everyone.

Their most notable achievement was a two-year effort, ending in 1996, to pass a health insurance reform bill that President Bill Clinton would sign. During the entire period, Kassebaum shepherded the bill through the Republican majority, rewriting it to meet objections while retaining Kennedy's priorities. The bill, popularly called "Kassebaum-Kennedy," was an attempt to enact some of President Clinton's reforms after his comprehensive health reform bill of 1994 ended in failure.

Kassebaum-Kennedy provided health insurance portability, meaning it allowed workers who changed jobs to bring their health insurance to the new company. It set up a pilot program of creating medical savings accounts—tax-free accounts that clients with high-deductible health insurance can use to pay medical expenses. It also raised the amount of health insurance premiums that self-employed people can deduct from their income tax. It prevented insurance companies from denying health coverage because of preexisting health conditions. And, it provided tax relief for those who buy insurance for long-term care.

Even this limited bill was controversial. Health insurance companies objected to a provision that required them to sell individual policies to people leaving group plans. They believed that people choosing this option were more likely to use their insurance, thus raising the companies' costs. This was later made more flexible. And

Kassebaum agreed with the argument that the bill might raise people's insurance premiums but said it was worth the tradeoff.

Kassebaum-Kennedy began with broad support but finally stalled in 1995 because of amendments that were considered too extreme. In 1996, the president endorsed the bill in his State of the Union Address. By doing so, he made the bill more important and put pressure on the Republican leadership to bring it to a vote.

Approval of a similar bill in the House met some resistance from Kennedy. Finally, a conference committee agreed on an acceptable bill. The president signed it into law in August 1996. It was Kassebaum's final piece of major legislation in the Senate.

She officially retired at the end of 1996; however, since then she has been appointed to head high-level bipartisan advisory panels covering the controversial subjects of campaign reform and single-sex military training. Her retirement ended the Landon political story in Kansas, but perhaps not on the national scene.

Kassebaum (center) carries an autographed basketball as she meets with assistant coach Renee Brown (second from left) and members of the USA Basketball Women's National Team, in 1995. Senator Dianne Feinstein (right) waits her turn. (AP/World Wide Photos)

Chronology

JULY 29, 1932	Nancy Landon is born in Topeka, Kansas
1952	receives B.A. from the University of Kansas
1955	receives M.A. from the University of Michigan
1956	marries Philip Kassebaum
1956–75	has four children—Philip Jr., Linda, Richard, and William—and raises them on their farm near Maize, Kansas; works as vice president of a family-owned company; serves as member and president of Maize School Board; serves on the Kansas Governmental Ethics Commission; serves on the Kansas Committee for the Humanities
1975	obtains a legal separation from husband
1975	becomes a caseworker in Washington, D.C., office of Senator James Pearson, assisting Kansans with government agencies
1978	Senator Pearson retires; Kassebaum runs for his seat and is elected to the U.S. Senate
1979	divorces Philip Kassebaum
1980	becomes member of the Senate Foreign Relations Committee
1984, 1990	is reelected to the U.S. Senate
1992	cofounds Republican Majority Coalition, whose purpose is to counteract the importance of the religious right in the Republican party

| 1994 | becomes first woman to chair a major Senate committee (Labor and Human Resources) |
| 1996 | retires from U.S. Senate |

Further Reading

"Nancy Landon Kassebaum." *Current Biography Yearbook.* Bronx, N.Y.: H.W. Wilson, 1982. Sketch of the early part of Kassebaum's career.

"Student Loan Programs Targeted." *CQ Almanac 1995,* Washington, D.C.: Congressional Quarterly, Section 8, p. 9. Discussion of student loan legislation, including Kassebaum's role.

"Moderates Refuse to Slip Quietly Away." *CQ Almanac 1995,* Washington, D.C.: Congressional Quarterly, Section 1, p. 17. Discussion of the legislative priorities of Kassebaum and other moderate Republican senators.

"Health Insurance Bill Stalls in Senate." *CQ Almanac 1995,* Washington, D.C.: Congressional Quarterly, Section 7, p. 24. Status report on the Kassebaum-Kennedy health reform bill.

"Lawmakers Aim to Consolidate Job Training Programs." *CQ Almanac 1995,* Washington, D.C.: Congressional Quarterly, Section 8, p. 3. Discussion of the status of job training legislation.

"Bill Makes Health Insurance 'Portable.'" *CQ Almanac 1996,* Washington, D.C.: Congressional Quarterly, Section 6, p. 28. Final report on the Kassebaum-Kennedy health reform legislation.

The following web page provides biographical material:

http://www.vote-smart.org

Dianne Feinstein

(1933–)

On November 27, 1978, Dianne Feinstein, president of the San Francisco County Board of Supervisors, was working in her office in City Hall. Around midday she heard the unusual sound of someone running down the corridor. Through her partly open office door, she recognized a former supervisor running by with a gun in his hand. A second or two later she heard several shots.

Quickly looking into a nearby office, Feinstein saw Supervisor Harvey Milk lying on the floor, dead. A moment later, someone told her that Mayor George Moscone had also been shot to death.

San Francisco has a combined city-county government, and as head of the county's Board of Supervisors, Feinstein automatically became the city's new mayor. She had long wanted to be mayor, but through an election, not this way. Now, however, she had a chance to prove how good a mayor she could be.

Feinstein was born Dianne Goldman on June 22, 1933. On the surface, she was a privileged child, growing up in a wealthy San Francisco neighborhood. Her father, Leon Goldman, a surgeon and

Senator Dianne Feinstein in 1993 (AP/Wide World Photos)

teacher, was an observant Jew. Her mother, Betty Goldman, be-
longed to the Russian Orthodox Church. Dianne's education reflected her religious background. She attended a Jewish religious
school, but following her mother's wishes, went to high school at the
Roman Catholic Convent of the Sacred Heart, graduating in 1951.

Dianne Goldman grew up with diverse political views due to the
opposing beliefs of her conservative Republican father and her liberal

> *I decided to run for elected office in 1969 because I believed . . . that elected office is where I can make the greatest contribution and can provide the most help for people who need assistance in solving real problems.*
>
> —Dianne Feinstein

uncle Morris Goldman who sometimes lived with Dianne's family. The two men had frequent political discussions that Dianne would listen to. Morris Goldman introduced her to the San Francisco of blue-collar workers and the disadvantaged, and took her to the Board of Supervisors meetings.

This diverse background was excellent training for a future politician. But Dianne's childhood also contained a tragic element; she was an abused child, growing up with an alcoholic and emotionally disturbed mother.

Dianne tried her best to control her mother's behavior by adding water to liquor bottles and by keeping her two younger sisters away from their mother as much as she could. She was often the victim of her mother's physical and emotional attacks. Dianne spent the night before her College Board exams sleeping in the family car because her mother had locked her out of the house. Despite this, she did well enough on the exams to be accepted by Stanford University.

Dianne Goldman won her first election at Stanford—as student body vice president. After graduating in 1955 with a B.A. in history, she continued her public affairs training for a year with a fellowship to study the criminal justice system. She then served as an intern with the Industrial Welfare Commission, and later she worked for the San Francisco district attorney's office for a year. Along the way she became a Democrat.

Also in 1955, she married a prosecuting attorney, Jack Berman. Three years later, the marriage ended, leaving her a single mother with an infant daughter, Katherine. The marriage also left her with a hearty dislike of the homemaker's role that her husband had urged her to accept.

Her political ambitions were boosted by chance. One of her convent friends was a daughter of California's then attorney general, Edmund G. "Pat" Brown. In 1960 Brown, now governor of California, decided to reform the Women's Board of Prisons and Paroles, which set sentences for female prisoners. He appointed several younger women to the board; one of them was Dianne Goldman. Over the next five years, Goldman made decisions at more than 5,000 parole hearings. This experience formed the basis for her "tough on crime" opinion in future years.

Newly elected San Francisco County Supervisor Feinstein in 1969. As the top vote-getter, she became president of the Board of Supervisors. (AP/Wide World Photos)

In 1962, she married neurosurgeon Bertram Feinstein. He adopted her daughter, and she took his name. Her new husband supported her political ambitions, and his long hours of work allowed Dianne Feinstein the time to pursue politics. In 1970, she ran successfully for a seat on the county Board of Supervisors.

As the top vote-getter among all supervisors running in the election, Feinstein automatically became president of the Board of Supervisors. She continued to be reelected through 1978, also serving as president from 1974 to 1975 and in 1978. A supervisor's job was important but unglamorous, involving basic services, such as making sure the trash is collected. By 1978 it was no longer enough to satisfy Feinstein's political aspirations. She wanted a more prestigious job. Only the mayor of San Francisco fit that description. The problem was, she had already run for mayor twice, losing by wide margins both times.

So in 1978, she came to a turning point in her career. For months she examined her choices. Should she run for mayor again? Should she run for supervisor again? Should she retire from politics? Making a decision like this is hard for any politician, but it was especially hard for Feinstein whose husband had died earlier that year after a long battle with cancer; she was exhausted and still in mourning. Finally, she made up her mind. Early on November 27, 1978, she told reporters her decision: She wasn't going to run for political office again.

A few hours later, an emotionally overwrought, 32-year-old former supervisor named Daniel White changed Feinstein's political life. White had recently resigned from the Board of Supervisors, then changed his mind and asked Mayor Moscone to appoint him to his old seat. Moscone, however, had already decided to replace him and planned to announce his choice later that day. White asked the mayor to meet with him, went to Moscone's offices and shot him four times. He then went to the supervisors' offices. Supervisor Harvey Milk tried to calm him, but White shot him five times and then fled the building. Less than an hour later, White surrendered at a police station. White was eventually convicted and sentenced to prison.

The city was already reeling after the mass murder-suicides of 900 members of a local cult in Jonestown, Guyana, a week earlier, and word of the assassinations of Mayor Moscone and Supervisor Milk spread quickly. At a hastily called press conference, Feinstein walked down City Hall's front steps to the microphones and solemnly told the public about the double murder.

As San Francisco's new leader, Feinstein knew she must be in charge from the beginning. That wasn't hard for her, since being in control of things was her natural style, but this situation was unusual. First, the killer was a former politician. And, even though the murder of the popular mayor Moscone was bad enough, the other victim, Harvey Milk, was San Francisco's first openly gay elected official and an honored figure in the city's large, politically active gay community.

Feinstein had to complete three tasks immediately: She had to make sure that the police department was handling the murder investigation promptly and correctly. At the same time, she had to convince the public that the government continued to function. Touchiest of all, she had to assure the gay community that Milk's death was not part of an antigay conspiracy. Within the next few weeks, Mayor Feinstein successfully completed all three.

Feinstein continued governing to the public's satisfaction, being reelected until 1988. She even survived a 1983 recall campaign—a citizen-initiated call for a special election to remove her from office—started by people opposed to her gun control efforts. She won with 80 percent of the vote. In 1987, *City and State Magazine* gave her the "All Pro Management Team" Award for No. 1 mayor.

Solidly supporting her was her third husband, Richard Blum, an investment banker whom she had married in 1980. In fact, Blum was also one of Feinstein's political advisors and fund-raisers.

Still, after all those years as mayor, she started thinking about other political jobs. She decided to run for governor of California in 1990 on the Democratic ticket. There was one problem: She didn't have a statewide political organization. She and Blum finally had to lend her campaign $3 million (She was later fined $190,000 by the California Fair Political Practices Commission for this.) Her late start in organizing may have cost her the election to Republican U.S. Senator Pete Wilson, another moderate.

With her statewide campaign organization, she turned her attention to the next major race—the 1992 election for the final two years

> *I believe that government is best conducted from the center of the political spectrum. What is important . . . is to listen to both sides . . ., make the decision, and move on to the next one.*
>
> —Dianne Feinstein

of Wilson's Senate term now that he was governor. On January 13, 1991, Feinstein announced her candidacy for this "short seat."

This time she ran a more traditionally feminist campaign than she had in the past. Another Democrat, U.S. Representative Barbara Boxer, was running for the "long senate seat," which was a full term left vacant by a retiring senator. The two often campaigned together stressing issues of major concern to women, such as health and education. The image of two women running for Senate seats also appealed to TV news cameras.

Feinstein won her nomination easily, as did Barbara Boxer, and Feinstein seemed to catch fire with their victories. "The status quo has got to go," she shouted at her June 8, 1992, victory celebration in San Francisco. With a big lead in the public opinion polls, she easily won her Senate seat.

She was part of a great Democratic sweep in the fall elections. Bill Clinton had won the presidential race. Boxer had also won. For the first time in U.S. history, both senators for a given state were women. Feinstein became California's senior senator, sworn in as soon as the election results were verified. (Boxer was sworn in when the new congress convened, in January.) She plunged into her new job with her almost relentless attention to detail and her priorities of nonpartisanship and a strict anticrime agenda. But, she also had to start campaigning again almost at once. In just two years she would have to run for office again, this time for a full six-year senate term.

In politics, an incumbent—the person who holds the office—is supposed to have the advantage, so it's usually easier to win the next election. Feinstein wasn't so lucky. The great Democratic wave of 1992 had turned into a Republican tide in 1994.

Unlike her first campaign, which was issue-oriented, this one was almost entirely negative, each candidate concentrating on the other's financial practices. Feinstein finally won a narrow victory. Still, her close call was a Democratic bright spot in an election in which the Republicans took control of both houses of Congress. Her reelection to a full term gave her increased power in the Senate and in the Democratic party.

In 1997, Feinstein served on three Senate committees: Judiciary, Foreign Affairs, and Rules and Administration. That same year, her Democratic colleagues named her ranking minority member—meaning that she would be chairperson if the Democrats regained the majority—of the Judiciary Committee's Subcommittee on Technology, Government Information, and Terrorism. This gave her much influence over laws relating to technological issues, such as security in computer transactions and electronic privacy, which are important in California's large high-tech industry. Being the ranking member also increased her influence on antiterrorism enforcement.

Feinstein was also the ranking Democratic member of the Foreign Relations Committee's Near Eastern and South Asian Affairs Subcommittee.

She is still tough on crime and continues to stress mediation and consensus-building on polarizing issues. During the 1995–96 Congress she cowrote and led the floor fight for passage of the Comprehensive Methamphetamine Control Act of 1996, which increases prison sentences for "meth" dealers. Other laws that she wrote have helped make public schools more gun-free, have tightened restrictions on illegal immigrants, and have protected large stretches of California's desert lands.

> *The essential qualities of leadership are the ability to make a decision. The courage to press that decision. The ability to understand when one has made a mistake and not to make the same mistake twice.*
>
> —Dianne Feinstein

In the 1995–96 Congress, Feinstein and Republican senator Orrin Hatch from Utah wrote a bill to strengthen federal antigang laws by doubling prison sentences for drive-by shootings and making it a federal crime to recruit minors into a gang. The bill didn't pass in that congressional session. But on the first day of the 1997 session, Hatch, who was chairman of the Judiciary Committee, reintroduced the bill, now called the Federal Gang Violence Act of 1997. Feinstein has made passing it one of her top priorities.

She has also been a longtime supporter of the rights of crime victims. Her victims' rights plan proposes a Constitutional amendment that increases the legal rights of victims of crime and their families. In 1996, she received an award from the National Association of Victims' Assistance for her work.

And she continues to stress women's issues. Early in 1997, she and two Republican senators wrote and introduced the Women's Health and Cancer Rights Act, which would let physicians and patients, rather than health insurance plans, determine the type of treatment and hospitalization needed for breast cancer sufferers. It would prevent so-called drive-through mastectomies—breast cancer operations performed on an out-patient basis, meaning the patient doesn't stay in the hospital overnight. Also, she urged the Senate to release money for international family planning projects.

Feinstein has been a leader in women's inclusion in government. She was the first woman vice president of the Stanford University student body, the first woman president of the San Francisco Board of Supervisors, the first woman mayor of San Francisco, the first woman to become a major party candidate for governor of California, the first woman to represent California in the U.S. Senate. After all this time, she says that what she likes best about her job is that she can make life better for people all across America.

Feinstein's next senatorial election comes in the year 2000.

Chronology

JUNE 22, 1933	Dianne Goldman is born, San Francisco, California
1951	graduates from the Convent of the Sacred Heart High School
1955	graduates from Stanford University, with a B.A. in history; wins a fellowship to study public affairs; marries Jack Berman, a prosecuting attorney
1957	gives birth to daughter Katherine
1958	divorces Jack Berman
1960–65	is appointed by Governor Edmund G. "Pat" Brown to serve on the Women's Board of Prisons and Paroles
1962	marries Bertram Feinstein, a neurosurgeon
1969	is elected to the San Francisco County Board of Supervisors; serves several times, three of them as president
1978	Bertram Feinstein dies of cancer
1978–88	Dianne Feinstein becomes mayor of the city of San Francisco, following the assassination of Mayor George Moscone
1980	marries Richard Blum, an investment banker

1990	runs unsuccessfully as Democratic candidate for governor of California; loses to Pete Wilson
1992	runs successfully to fill Pete Wilson's unexpired U.S. Senate term; becomes California's senior senator
1994	runs successfully for reelection to a full six-year term in the U.S. Senate

Further Reading

Lesher, Dave. "Huffington Wins Bid to Challenge Feinstein." *Los Angeles Times,* June 8, 1994, pp. A3, A16. Overview of Feinstein's second senatorial primary victory.

———. "Doubts on Feinstein's Support Rewrites Odds." *Los Angeles Times,* June 9, 1994, p. 1. Analysis of Feinstein's upcoming general election campaign.

Lesher, Dave, and Glenn F. Bunting. "Feinstein Is Apparent Winner in Senate Race." *Los Angeles Times,* November 10, 1994, p. 1. Analysis of Feinstein's narrow win in her second senatorial campaign.

Lesher, Dave, and Greg Krikorian. "Bitterly Fought Senate Race Too Close to Call." *Los Angeles Times,* November 9, 1994, pp. 1, A20. Recapitulation of Feinstein's second senate race.

Lodop, Laurie. *Political Leaders.* New York: Twenty-First Century Books, 1996.

Morin, Isabel V. *Women of the U.S. Congress.* Minneapolis, Minn.: Oliver Press, Inc., 1994.

Morris, Celia. *Storming the Statehouse: Running for Governor with Ann Richards and Dianne Feinstein.* New York: Charles Scribner's Sons, 1992. A behind-the-scenes examination of Feinstein's 1990 race for governor. The book contains much biographical material, plus a photographic section.

Pollack, Jill S. *Women on the Hill: A History of Women in Congress.* New York: Franklin Watts, 1996. A young adult book that surveys women in Congress.

Stall, Bill, and Tracy Wilkinson. "California Gets Its First Woman Senator." *Los Angeles Times,* November 4, 1992, pp. 1, A14. Recapitulation of Feinstein's first senatorial election.

Wilkinson, Tracy, and Bill Stall. "Feinstein, Boxer Win Easily." *Los Angeles Times,* June 3, 1992, pp. 1, A14. Description of Feinstein's first senatorial primary victory.

Wilkinson, Tracy, and Dean E. Murphy. "Candidates for Senate Hold Final Rallies." *Los Angeles Times,* November 3, 1992, pp. 1, A3. Overview of Feinstein's general election campaign in 1992.

Biographical material is found on the following web pages:

http://www.senate.gov/member/ca/feinstein/general
http://www.vote-smart.org

Ann Richards

(1933–)

The year was 1975. Ann Richards was a wife, mother of four, and a homemaker in Austin, Texas. She had worked on campaigns and done political organizing for years, always getting her husband's approval first. She had always seen herself as his helper. She had even run a successful campaign for a state representative, Sarah Weddington. Now, a group of progressive Democrats wanted her husband to run for county commissioner. His response surprised her. He didn't want to run. Instead, he said to her, why don't *you* run?

She wasn't sure being an elected official suited her. She loved being involved in a campaign but was always glad when it was over. Also, many Texans thought a woman couldn't handle a job that included finances, road maintenance, and supervising the sheriff's office. It would be a full-time job away from her family all day. Worst of all, she feared if she won the election and performed well, it might disrupt her 22-year marriage; it might even end it. She decided to turn the job down, but her husband talked her into running.

Dorothy Ann Willis was born on September 1, 1933, in Lakeview, Texas, an only child. Her parents, Cecil and Iona Warren Willis came from very poor, rural families. Cecil Willis was born in a small community outside Lorena, Texas, named Bugtussle. He quit high school before graduating so that he could get a job to help support the family. He worked for the same company all his adult life, beginning as a truck driver and ending as a salesman. Iona Warren Willis came from the vicinity of Hico, Texas, south of Ft. Worth, but moved to Waco, where she was a saleswoman in a dry goods store when she and Cecil met on a blind date.

Ann—she dropped the Dorothy when she entered high school—was born in a tiny house the Willises bought in Lakeview. The day she gave birth, Iona Willis, still in bed, wrung the neck of a chicken so that her husband would have something to eat when he returned home from work.

Texas governor Ann Richards testifies before the Senate Environment and Public Works Committee in 1993, during hearings on environmental improvements along the U.S.-Mexico border. (AP/Wide World Photos)

Both parents were ambitious for their only child, despite their modest circumstances during the Great Depression. Iona made nice clothes for Ann and saw to it that she took music and recitation lessons. Her father told her that she could do anything she wanted with her life if she worked hard enough. After Ann graduated from junior high school in Lakeview, the family moved to Waco so that she could have a better education.

Her best subjects at Waco High School were English and speech—perhaps a family trait; her father was a great storyteller. Ann joined the debate team, which won the girls' state championship her senior year. Mostly on the basis of this, she was selected to represent her school at Girls State, a national program in which girls formed a mock government, held elections, and passed laws in the legislature. Since there were almost no female elected officials in the late 1940s, the experience was primarily educational. But Ann enjoyed it and was selected as one of two Texans to attend Girls Nation (the next level of the program) in Washington, D.C. There, she met one of the few women holding a high federal position, Georgia Neese Clark, treasurer of the United States. And, she shook hands with President Harry Truman in the Rose Garden.

After graduating from high school in 1950, she attended Baylor University. She married David Richards, her high school boyfriend, in 1953, after her junior year. She graduated in 1954 with a degree in history.

The couple moved to Austin, where David enrolled in the University of Texas Law School. Ann earned a teaching certificate in 1955 and taught social studies in area schools for two years. For the next 20 years, she happily played the then-common woman's roles of housewife, mother, and volunteer, while David worked as a labor lawyer in Dallas and then in Austin. Eventually the Richardses had four children: Cecile, Clark, Dan, and Ellen.

The Texas Democratic party in the 1960s was divided into two camps. One group was extremely conservative and favored segregation. The other, less powerful one, was more liberal. Both Ann and David Richards were aligned with this liberal wing. She worked part-time in the John F. Kennedy–Lyndon B. Johnson presidential campaign in 1960. After Kennedy's election, David was appointed staff attorney in the Civil Rights Commission, in Washington, D.C. In 1962, the family moved back to Texas.

Richards soon became more active politically, organizing a group of like-minded women into an organization called the North Dallas Democratic Women. The group had two purposes: to have some power in the male-dominated Democratic organization and to elect liberal Democrats to office. Also in the 1960s, Ann and David founded the Dallas Committee for Peaceful Integration, an organization designed to help end racial segregation in the public schools.

Richards suffered from a series of illnesses during the 1960s—high blood pressure, a life-threatening pregnancy with their fourth child, and grand mal epileptic seizures. When she recovered, the Richardses moved to the more progressive and intellectual city of Austin, where David relocated his law practice.

Richards had decided to give up further political activity because there appeared little chance that women would be allowed real power. But in 1971, a friend introduced her to a 26-year-old lawyer named Sarah Weddington, who needed professional help in running for the state legislature. Weddington was the lawyer who won the abortion rights case, *Roe* v. *Wade,* before the Supreme Court. Richards was impressed with her practical approach to political life and her women's rights agenda, and decided to help her.

The successful campaign was a turning point in Richards's life. After 15 years of marriage, working on the Weddington campaign was the first major action she had taken on her own. For the first time, David helped Ann, not the other way around, as it had always been in the past.

Richards became Weddington's administrative assistant in 1974 for one legislative session. That same year, she was asked to help another woman, Wilhelmina Delco, become Austin's first African-American representative—another successful campaign for Richards.

The next year, Richards herself won her first election, unseating an incumbent county commissioner by a two-to-one margin. In office, she concentrated on better funding for women's services, creating a shelter for battered women, and streamlining governmental operations. Later, in other offices, she would continue her efforts on both issues.

At the same time, she became committed to the growing women's rights movement nationally, as well as in Texas. She was one of the few high profile women in elected office—one of just 18 female Texas county commissioners, compared to almost 1,000 men. Less than 1 percent of Texas's judges were women. Even on school boards, less than 10 percent of the members were women.

In 1977, she made a speech favoring the Equal Rights Amendment at a gathering of 20,000 women in Houston. In 1978, she attended the National Women's Educational Fund session in Aspen, Colorado, for elected women. She joined the National Women's Political Caucus and started being known for her witty speeches, which were rewarded with applause and votes. She traveled the state collecting material for the Texas Women's Archive—a historical display of the contribution to Texas history made by women of all races. And, as a county commissioner, for the first time she was making important decisions without asking her husband what she should do. It was an eye-opener for her.

Recognizing her strength as a woman didn't come easily to Richards. At first, she told herself her activities were mainly for her two daughters, as she realized the greater advantages her sons received in school. But finally she looked at herself in the mirror and admitted that she was doing this for herself, too.

Following this new path wasn't easy. The pressures of her public role pushed her from a social drinker to an alcoholic. Finally, in 1980, her husband and a group of friends held an intervention and convinced her to get help. While spending a month in a Minnesota alcoholism treatment center, she stopped drinking. She has been a member of Alcoholics Anonymous ever since.

Her new career took her and David on separate paths. After several separations, they finally divorced in 1984.

In 1981, a candidate for governor asked her to run for state treasurer. After discussing it with friends, she decided that if she could raise $200,000 in campaign pledges in 24 hours, she would run. The pledges came in. She ran for treasurer and won with over 60 percent of the vote. She was the first woman in 50 years to win a statewide office in Texas.

She soon discovered that the treasurer's office was decades behind the times. It was inefficient in handling money, often letting it sit for weeks before going into a bank account. The state deposited its money in dozens of low-interest bank accounts all over Texas. The vast majority of its employees were white males. Richards changed all that.

She hired minority members and women with up-to-date skills so that the staff better represented the state's population. She streamlined the deposit system, putting money into higher-interest accounts the day it was received and keeping it there until it was needed. During two terms as treasurer—she was reelected in 1986—she earned almost $2 billion more for the state than the old system would have brought in.

For her vote-winning ability and her style on the campaign trail, she became a rising star of the national Democratic party. In 1988, she became a celebrity after delivering the keynote speech at the Democratic National Convention. The speech blended progressive ideas with "down home" Texas style, good humor with the expected political bashing of wealthy Republican (and fellow Texan) President George Bush for backtracking on a "no new taxes" pledge. She won supporters throughout the country.

She immediately capitalized on this celebrity status by running for governor—a 2 ½ year ordeal. If she won, she wouldn't be Texas's first woman governor. In the 1920s and 1930s, Miriam A. "Ma" Ferguson served two terms as governor, as a stand-in for her husband, "Pa" Ferguson, who

P*oor George.*
He can't help it.
He was born with
a silver foot in
his mouth.

—Ann Richards

Texas state treasurer Richards is escorted across the state Capitol grounds, shortly after winning the Democratic nomination for governor in 1990. (AP/Wide World Photos)

was ineligible to run. "Pa" Ferguson's office was right next to his wife's, and she governed according to his wishes. But, Richards would be the first woman governor to run in her own right, and the first who was a liberal.

Richards's Republican opponent was Clayton Williams, a self-made businessman with a Texas-cowboy image. "Claytie" Williams's campaign was designed to appeal to rich, conservative voters like himself. But it also appealed to the cowboy spirit that lies deep inside most Texans, regardless of their economic situation and where they were born and raised.

Richards has always evoked Texas's rural past, complete with the earthy humor and small-town friendliness that comes naturally to her. The issues of governing were less important than style, mostly because the Texas governor has much less power than governors of most states. Most of the power is held by commissions whose members' terms expire on a staggered basis. This means that the governor must often compromise with commission members who were elected with the support of an earlier governor of a different political party.

In the end, Richards narrowly won the governor's race for two reasons. First, she talked specifically about her successes in the treasurer's office and proved herself better informed than Williams. And second, Williams broke his own "cowboy code" by being unchivalrous to a woman—he refused to shake Richards's hand at a public meeting. In the end, more people disliked him than disliked Richards. She defeated Williams by less than three percentage points. A third candidate, a Libertarian, got a little more than 3 percent of the vote.

As she did in the treasurer's office, Richards broadened the range of people she appointed. In her first year, almost half of these were women, one-fourth were Hispanic, and 12 percent were African Americans. She brought clean, running water to the people who lived in impoverished settlements—called "colonias"—near the Mexican border. She included drug treatment facilities in the new prisons being built. She tightened regulation of the insurance industry, increased coverage, and lowered rates. As always, she was strongly pro-choice, promising to veto any antiabortion bill the legislature passed. She also supported passage of an antistalking bill.

Richards's term as governor also had several failures. First, her political power as head of the Texas Democratic party was unexpectedly weakened. The man she appointed to replace Democratic senator Lloyd Bentsen, who had resigned to serve in President Bill Clinton's cabinet, was defeated in a special election by Republican Kay Bailey Hutchison. Senator Hutchison later won a full six-year term.

Governor Richards tried to develop a plan to finance court-ordered equalization of funding for all school districts. A referendum on her plan defeated it. Instead, she had to reach an exhausting compromise with the legislature. She signed the bill just one day before all the schools would have been forced to close.

Also, the federal government closed down a futuristic science project being built in Texas, the Super Conducting Supercollider, which Richards had strongly supported.

In 1994, many expected her to win reelection. But in a year of Republican victories nationwide, she was defeated by Republican George W. Bush, son of former president George Bush, who took

Former Texas governor Richards in 1996 (AP/Wide World Photos)

53 percent of the vote. Richards ran well, but later analysis of voter profiles showed she couldn't overcome the gender gap—men voted more strongly for Bush than women did for her. She became the latest in a line of Texas governors turned out of office after a single term.

This is not the end of the world," she told her supporters. "It is the end of a campaign." However, Richards did not run for office again.

In late 1997, in what may be her most controversial political move yet, Richards became a paid lobbyist for the tobacco industry. She is urging members of Congress to support a bill that would limit the amount of money that people with smoking-related illnesses can claim in lawsuits. The proposed legislation supports an agreement between state attorneys general and leading tobacco companies.

Chronology

SEPTEMBER 1, 1933	Dorothy Ann Willis is born in Lakeview, Texas
1950	graduates from high school in Waco
1953	marries David Richards
1954	graduates from Baylor University with a B.A. in history
1954–71	raises four children: Cecile, Clark, Dan, and Ellen; volunteers in several peace and women's political groups
1971	works part-time as a campaign organizer for state legislature candidate Sarah Weddington
1974	works as Weddington's administrative assistant; advises another legislative candidate, Wilhelmina Delco, on her successful campaign
1975	is elected a county supervisor
1978	collects material for the Texas Women's Archive
1982	runs for state treasurer and wins
1984	divorces David Richards
1986	is reelected state treasurer

1988	gives keynote address at Democratic National Convention
1990	runs for governor and is elected
1994	is defeated in her campaign for reelection

Further Reading

Abramson, Jill, and Barry Meier. "Tobacco Braced for Costly Fight." *New York Times,* December 15, 1997, p. A1. Analysis of the role of lobbyists, such as Richards, in the congressional fight shaping up over limitation of liability for tobacco companies.

Lodop, Laurie. *Political Leaders.* New York: Twenty-First Century Books, 1996.

Morris, Celia. *Storming the Statehouse: Running for Governor with Ann Richards and Dianne Feinstein.* New York: Charles Scribner's Sons, 1992. A behind-the-scenes examination of Richards's 1990 race for governor. The book contains much biographical material, plus a photographic section.

Richards, Ann, with Peter Knobler. *Straight From the Heart: My Life in Politics and Other Places.* New York: Simon & Schuster, 1989. Richards pulls no punches in this warmly-told autobiography. She includes background on her political campaigns, her search for herself as an individual, her alcoholism, and her family.

Schropshire, Mike. *The Thorny Rose of Texas: An Intimate Portrait of Gov. Ann Richards.* Secaucus, N.J.: Carol Pub. Group, 1994. This book is mainly a rehash of Richards's autobiography, but has some updated material.

Siegel, Dorothy S. *Ann Richards: Politician, Feminist Survivor.* Springfield, N.J.: Enslow Publishers, Inc., 1996.

Tolleson-Rinehart, Sue. *Claytie and the Lady: Ann Richards, Gender, and Politics in Texas.* Austin, Tex.: University of Texas Press, 1994. Tolleson-Rinehart analyzes Richards's governor's campaign in the context of Texas history, other Texas political battles, and the psychology of Clayton Williams as a male Texan. A bit long in places, but a good story told in academic style.

Geraldine Ferraro

(1935–)

The new vice presidential candidate of the Democratic party gazed out at an audience of 10,000 National Convention delegates. Waves of the chant "Ger-ry, Ger-ry" filled the Moscone Center in San Francisco. Geraldine Ferraro began to speak. "Tonight the daughter of an immigrant from Italy has been chosen to run for vice president in the new land my father came to love."

She was already a three-term congresswoman. That night, July 19, 1984, Ferraro became the highest-ranking female political candidate in United States history. Never before or since has a woman been chosen as the vice presidential candidate of a major political party. It was, she said, a powerful signal to all Americans.

Geraldine Anne Ferraro was born in Newburgh, New York, on August 26, 1935. Her father, Dominick Ferraro, was an immigrant from Italy and the owner of a restaurant in this small city north of Manhattan. Her mother, Antonetta Corrieri Ferraro, a seamstress,

Former representative Geraldine Ferraro says she is "addicted to politics."
(AP/Wide World Photos)

was of Italian descent. Tragedy had already visited the family twice before Geraldine's birth. Of their three sons, one had died in infancy. Another, named Girard, was killed in an automobile accident as he lay asleep in his mother's lap. For the next year, Antonetta Ferraro was so distracted by this death that she spent all her time washing and ironing the child's clothes. The family's doctor finally suggested that she could get past this grief by having another child. A daughter was born the next year, weighing a hefty 10-plus pounds. Her parents named her Geraldine, after the child who had died.

Geraldine's parents wanted the best for her and their remaining son Carl, especially in education. Both parents worked and sacrificed so that their children could attend private schools. When Geraldine was eight, her father suddenly died of a heart condition that he had concealed from the rest of the family. Geraldine and her father had been very close, and his death devastated her.

Her mother moved the family back to her old New York City neighborhood of Queens, to be near her relatives. She was determined to continue her plans for their children. She worked as a seamstress, crocheting beads into fancy patterns for women's dresses. You can do anything, she told Geraldine: *Ferro* means "iron" in Italian and is the root of the family name. Iron bends, but it doesn't break, her mother reminded her. One of the lessons Geraldine drew from her mother's advice was always to have a backup for any plan that she made—a process she has followed throughout her life.

Geraldine attended a Roman Catholic school and was bright enough to skip the seventh and eighth grades. She graduated from Marymount School in nearby Tarrytown, New York, in 1952, at the age of 16. She entered Marymount Manhattan College, in New York City, on a full scholarship, graduating with a B.A. in English. At the same time, she took classes at Hunter College, to earn a teaching certificate. All through college, she earned expense money by working as a saleswoman at Bloomingdale's, an exclusive department store.

The fall after graduation, she started teaching second grade in the New York City public schools. At the same time, she enrolled in nearby Fordham University's law school, taking night courses for the next four

> T*here are no doors we cannot unlock. We will place no limits on achievement. If we do this, we can do anything.*
>
> —Geraldine Ferraro

years. She was one of just two women in her class of 200, and the university's president, a friend, sternly told her she was taking a place that a man would ordinarily fill—a common attitude in those days.

In 1960, when she was about to receive her law degree with honors, Ferraro also sensed this message when being interviewed, and not hired, by law firms. The law firms' attitudes were reinforced when she told them she planned to get married right after graduation. They expected that once married, a woman didn't want or need a job.

That summer she married her boyfriend of several years, John Zaccaro, who worked with his father in their real estate investment firm. She kept her own name, in honor of her mother. Later that year, she passed the bar examination and, in 1961, she was admitted to the New York City bar, allowing her to practice law.

For the next 14 years, Ferraro's time was mainly devoted to her family life. She had three children: Donna, born in 1962; John Jr., in 1964; and Laura, in 1966. As John Zaccaro's business prospered, the family moved to an exclusive neighborhood and joined an expensive tennis club. The children went to prestigious prep schools, and they all spent holidays at their vacation home in the Caribbean.

Ferraro practiced law part-time and once worked on the political campaign of her cousin Nicholas Ferraro, when he ran (unsuccessfully) for the state senate. She also worked on several neighborhood zoning issues and became better known in the area.

By 1974, Ferraro was ready for a full-time career. She asked Nicholas Ferraro, who was now the Queens district attorney, for a job. After she was approved by his screening committee, he appointed her an assistant prosecutor. Her opponents were accused rapists and those who abused children and the elderly. After several years, she felt burned out by this work but had been deeply moved by the injustices in society that led to many of these cases.

She also discovered the extent of discrimination against women lawyers. The bar examination was given to men and women separately. Criminal law was considered "men's work," and some district attorneys refused to hire any women. She also discovered that she was being paid less than the male attorneys in her office. "You don't need the money," she was told. Women were not even allowed to join the Queens County Bar Association.

She had always intended to seek political office as a Democrat. In 1978, her district's 16-term representative retired and Ferraro decided to run for the job. The political organization refused to enter her name in the primary, so she got on the ballot the hard way: Ferraro, her husband, and a few friends gathered signatures throughout the neighborhood, until she had enough to qualify for the ballot.

Using $234,000 borrowed (legally, she believed) from her husband, she beat two opponents in the primary with 53 percent of the vote. Shortly before the primary election, the Federal Election Commission told her that she had exceeded the individual limitation of $1,000 in contributions or loans. She then sold some of her own real estate and repaid the loan. Her explanation was unconvincing to some people, however, and this and other financial practices would haunt her electoral career from then on. For example, her husband refused to make his tax returns public, giving the impression that there was something to hide. Also, she was an officer in his business but claimed not to know anything about Zaccaro's financial dealings. This too gave the appearance of deception.

Her main campaign issue was a seemingly small matter that was very important in her district. Several neighborhoods shared postal zip codes with the neighboring borough of Brooklyn, forcing them to share Brooklyn's higher auto, home, and life insurance rates. If they had Queens-based zip codes, the rates would be lower. Ferraro promised that, if the voters elected her, she would get the zip codes changed.

She won the election. In the House of Representatives, she was assigned to the Post Office and Civil Service Committee—a typical beginner's assignment—and promptly succeeded in having the zip codes changed. She admits that at first she was a conservative Democrat from a conservative district made up mostly of blue-collar Italians and Roman Catholics, but with some high-income sections. She became more liberal as her career continued.

After winning a seat on the House Budget Committee, she began to specialize in championing legislation that protected children, women, and senior citizens—a pattern that continued through her career in the House of Representatives. She was especially active in writing and voting for legislation that improved women's economic

T o those concerned about the strength of family values as I am, I say: We are going to restore those values—love, caring, partnership—by including, and not excluding, those whose beliefs differ from our own.

—Geraldine Ferraro

status, such as allowing homemakers to contribute to spouses' pensions and individual retirement accounts.

Another pattern that continued through the 1980s was her political opposition to the policies of Republican President Ronald Reagan, who was first elected in 1980. And in addition to taking on social issues, Ferraro was an environmentalist.

One of her positions, however, was unpopular in her district—her support of a woman's freedom to choose an abortion. It also conflicted with the teachings of the Roman Catholic Church. Ferraro, who as a Roman Catholic is personally opposed to abortion, maintained that she could not prevent its use by others whose religion did not oppose it. Many Roman Catholic politicians take this position, but Church leaders were unusually outspoken against Ferraro's position. The archbishop (later, cardinal) of New York and another bishop campaigned politically against her pro-choice position, even though open politicking by clergy is frowned on by the National Council of Catholic Bishops.

The abortion conflict continued throughout her political career. Despite the controversy, she was reelected in 1980 with 58 percent of the vote and in 1982 with 73 percent.

Ferraro was also becoming well known as a superstar in the national Democratic party. In 1980, President Jimmy Carter named her national deputy chairman of the Carter-Mondale reelection drive. At the 1980 Democratic convention, she chaired the Credentials Committee. That same year she was elected secretary of the House Democratic Caucus, the main organization for Democrats in the House of Representatives. In 1981, she was named to a party committee that decided how delegates should be chosen for the 1984 convention. Later, she chaired the 1984 Platform Committee, which drafted the party's principles for the presidential election.

By 1984, the women's movement had become an established political force. Women were entering the work force in record numbers. Its effect on the Democratic party was especially strong and activists were pressing the party for the inclusion of more women candidates and party officials. At the same time, African Americans and other minority groups were becoming more vocal and their leaders, especially the Reverend Jesse Jackson, also wanted to be included.

The party had not done well in the last presidential election; President Carter had been defeated for reelection by Ronald Reagan in 1980. In 1984, the Democratic candidate would be facing Reagan in his reelection bid. It was already obvious that Reagan had overwhelming popular support. The Democrats needed a pair of candidates with as wide a voter appeal as possible. Many important Democrats said that it was time to have a woman on the ballot. Polls showed that this move would be popular with voters. A woman would appeal to women voters of all races and to minority voters. Two of the major presidential contenders agreed—Representative Gary Hart from Colorado, who had support from younger voters, and Walter Mondale of Minnesota, who had been President Carter's vice president.

Mondale was very public in his screening process for possible vice presidential running mates. As the convention drew near, Ferraro was one of two women on his final list.

The selection process was demanding. The prospects were closely questioned about all aspects of their political and private lives. In the end, presidential candidate Mondale selected Geraldine Ferraro. For the first time in history, a major political party chose a woman for the nation's second-highest office.

The vice presidential race was different from Ferraro's congressional campaigns in two ways: She was a stranger to most parts of the country, and she was campaigning as part of a team. Also, she knew that even if she *did* attract more women and minority voters, in the end, it was the presidential candidate who counted with the people.

Mondale, like Ferraro, campaigned on issues of social justice. But President Ronald Reagan was known as the "Teflon president" because criticism slid right off him. People voted for him as much as for his policies.

Ferraro had two other problems. Her campaign spending and her husband's business finances were questioned. Some claimed Ferraro had hidden sources of campaign money from John Zaccaro's real estate firm. Ferraro denied the charge but constantly had to answer questions about it. Also, once again, her position on abortion created a split with the Roman Catholic Church.

On election day, the Mondale-Ferraro ticket was defeated. Disappointed, Ferraro withdrew from politics for a time, but in 1992, she ran for the Democratic nomination for U.S. senator. Again, her finances were a major issue. This time, she lost in the primary election.

Shortly after his inauguration in 1993, President Bill Clinton named Ferraro a delegate to a United Nations Human Rights Commission conference. Ferraro is now a political commentator on CNN and a managing partner in the New York office of a national law firm. She is also on the board of visitors of the Fordham University law school.

Vice presidential candidate Ferraro campaigning in Boston in 1984
(AP/Wide World Photos)

In January 1998, she entered the race to become the Democratic candidate for U.S. senator, hoping to face three-term Republican Alphonse D'Amato in the November 1998 elections. She immediately became the front-runner in the September primary contest with New York congressman Charles Shumer and Mark Green, the New York City public advocate. As in earlier campaigns, her own financial practices soon became a major issue.

Chronology

AUGUST 26, 1935	Geraldine Anne Ferraro is born, Newburgh, New York
1952	graduates from Marymount School, Tarrytown, New York
1956	graduates from Marymount College, New York City, with a B.A. in English; takes classes at Hunter College, New York City and receives teaching certificate; begins teaching in grade school in the New York public schools; enrolls in Fordham University (New York) Law School at night and becomes one of two women students in a class of about 200
1960	graduates from Fordham University Law School; marries John Zaccaro, a real estate developer; passes the Bar examination
1961	is admitted to the New York City Bar
1962–66	has three children: Donna, John, and Laura
1974	becomes assistant prosecutor in Queens, New York, District Attorney's office, in the special victims bureau
1978	is elected to Congress from the 9th District, New York

1980, 1982	is reelected to Congress
1984	is nominated for vice president of the United States; she and presidential candidate Walter Mondale are defeated
1992	loses in Democratic party primary for nomination as New York senatorial candidate
1993	is appointed by President Bill Clinton to United Nations Human Rights Commission Conference; becomes managing partner, New York office of Keck, Mahin & Cate law firm
1996	becomes a commentator on CNN
1998	announces she will run for the Democratic nomination for U.S. senator

Further Reading

Breslin, Rosemary, and Joshua Hammer. *Gerry! A Woman Making History.* Introduction by Gloria Steinem. New York: Pinnacle Books, 1984. Details Ferraro's involvement in the women's movement but skims over Ferraro's life. Its summary of her legislative record in Congress is useful. With photographs.

Ferraro, Geraldine. *Changing History: Women, Power, and Politics.* Preface by Ann Richards. Wakefield, R.I.: Moyer Bell, 1993. This book contains several of her recent major speeches on politically oriented topics.

Ferraro, Geraldine, with Linda Bird Francke. *Ferraro: My Story.* New York: Bantam Books, 1985. Ferraro's autobiography tells her personal story and also provides her version of her difficulties with campaign finances and her differences with the Roman Catholic Church.

Lodop, Laurie. *Political Leaders.* New York: Twenty-First Century Books, 1996.

Maxine Waters

(1938–)

The looting and the fires that leveled sections of Los Angeles in April 1992 began in outrage after four white policemen were found not guilty in the beating of an African-American motorist, Rodney King. The devastation centered on Representative Maxine Waters's district. She quickly returned home from Washington, D.C., to see the riots for herself. Some community leaders wanted her to walk the streets and tell the rioters to "cool it," as congressmen had done during the Watts Riots 27 years earlier.

Waters disagreed. She opposed violence but said the rioters were right. They were expressing their hopelessness that improvements were ever coming to their disadvantaged area.

She took their message and hers to newspapers, television talk shows, churches, and the business community. ABC News named her Person of the Week.

When the rioting ended four days later, she had become one of the leading national spokespeople for the poor, the oppressed, and the ignored.

Representative Maxine Waters in 1995, warning that African Americans will not support the Democratic party if it abandons affirmative action (AP/Wide World Photos)

☆☆☆

Maxine Carr was born in St. Louis, Missouri, on August 15, 1938, the daughter of Remus and Velma Moore Carr. Her parents divorced two years later, and Maxine moved with her mother to a series of housing projects. Mrs. Carr married several times during Maxine's childhood and was on welfare periodically. Waters believes that she developed her own strength from seeing her mother's determination to survive during those years.

Maxine took her first job at the age of 13, as a bus girl in a segregated restaurant, where she had to eat in the basement. Later, she worked in a factory. She continued her studies, though, and graduated from high school in 1956.

In 1956, she married Edward Waters and spent the next several years raising their two children, Edward and Karen. The job market in St. Louis was unpromising, so the Waterses decided to move to southern California, where they thought prospects were brighter.

Settling in the Watts section of Los Angeles, they discovered that jobs were scarce there too. Maxine Waters took a low-paying job in the garment industry, while her husband worked in a printing plant. Waters finally found a better job as a telephone operator but had to quit after suffering a miscarriage.

Waters's career took a new direction in 1966, when she discovered the new, federally-funded Head Start, an educational program for the children of low-income families. She became an assistant teacher in a Head Start school and later a supervisor of its volunteer teachers. Her success led her to another way of helping people—politics.

Waters became deeply involved in the political world and volunteered in several local and state elections. At the same time, her marriage broke up; she and Edward Waters were divorced in 1972.

By 1973, she was skilled enough to manage the successful political campaign of a Los Angeles City Council candidate, David S. Cunningham. After taking office, Cunningham named Waters his chief deputy. In this position, she developed a reputation as a tough-minded, outspoken politician. She also helped in the election of Tom Bradley, Los Angeles's first African-American mayor.

Her own elective career began in 1976, after a questionable maneuver by the long time assemblyman in her district, Leon Ralph. He secretly decided not to run for reelection, postponing the announcement until his chosen successor had registered as a candidate at the last minute. A political storm followed, and the secretary of state was forced to extend the deadline so that other candidates could also register. Waters decided to enter the race. Running as an outsider, she won an upset victory in the Democratic primary and then won the general election.

Some assemblymembers, knowing her reputation as a fiery politician, wanted to block Waters's possible disruptive influence in the legislature. In her view, they wanted to teach her—a black woman from Los Angeles—a lesson by trying to block her influence on legislation and in committees.

In spite of these difficulties, she immediately began to work for laws to increase the power of women and children, as well as of

African Americans and Hispanics. She continued to work for these groups throughout her years in the assembly.

In 1977, she married Sidney Williams, a former football player and a luxury car salesman and who currently is the U.S. ambassador to the Bahamas, a Caribbean nation.

ˈ In 1978, she was a founder of the Black Women's Forum, a Los Angeles organization designed to teach women how to empower themselves. She later founded Project Build, a program that works with young people in Los Angeles housing projects on job training and placement.

She sponsored a bill to provide four months of parental leave for new mothers without losing their jobs. The bill became law in 1978 but was overturned in the federal courts in 1984 because it discriminated against men.

Another bill that she sponsored kept the police from strip-searching people stopped for minor offenses, such as expired dog licenses and traffic tickets. Her bill passed but was vetoed by the governor. Many of the people who had been strip-searched were women and children, and by mobilizing women's groups, Waters pressured the governor to support a modified bill, which became law in 1984.

Waters was also the leader in preventing the investment of California state funds in South Africa, which was then ruled by a white-minority government. Introducing the bill six times during an eight-year period, she finally had it passed in 1986.

She helped pass legislation that increased opportunities for women- and minority-owned businesses to sell materials and services to state agencies. She supported lengthening jail sentences for drug dealers who carried weapons. Other bills supported business investment in inner-city neighborhoods and established child abuse prevention programs.

Waters broke new ground for women in the assembly. She was the first woman in state history to serve as the majority whip (the second in command after the majority leader) and the first to be named to the rules committee, which defines the rules for legislative procedures.

She has sometimes used pressure tactics to her own political benefit, offending friends and enemies alike. For instance, she had her district's boundaries redrawn to her advantage. Accused of acting in an "unfeminine" way, she responded, "that's the way the guys do it."

By 1989, Waters was ready to move from the state to the national scene. When the longtime congressman from her district retired that year, she ran for the seat, in what in 1998 is California's 35th district, and won the primary with 88 percent of the vote. She won the general election with 80 percent of the vote.

> [T he violence was]
> *a spontaneous*
> *reaction to a lot of*
> *alienation and*
> *frustration.*
>
> —Maxine Waters

She was assigned to the House Veterans Affairs Committee. One of her first acts was to criticize the staff's composition—all Caucasian—while more than one-quarter of service men and women were members of minority groups. The committee added two African Americans to the staff.

In Congress, Waters has continued to combine blunt speech and no-holds-barred tactics to pass laws important to her. She has been active in supporting four kinds of legislation—economic development, housing, veterans' rights, and health.

As a member of the House Banking and Financial Services Committee, she helped neighborhoods maintain banking services even though branches of major banks have closed. Her efforts have assured that in such cases, financial institutions will consult with the affected community to work toward providing alternative banking services. She has also helped make it easier for developing nations to repay money that they have borrowed from the United States.

In housing, she has helped create Youthbuild, a program to employ disadvantaged young people in modernizing low-income housing.

She helped create a Center for Women Veterans within the Department of Veterans' Affairs. The center coordinates programs and policies for the growing number of women veterans. She wrote legislation to provide more facilities for women at veterans' medical centers. The law also provides for including women in clinical trials at the medical centers.

She has introduced a bill to expand research on heart attacks, stroke, and high blood pressure in women. In addition, the bill would create outreach programs to educate doctors and the public about cardiovascular disease—the leading killer of women.

Waters's outspoken manner has sometimes led people to assume that she is an outsider in the political world. The opposite is true. Waters has played an active role in the Democratic party, sitting on the Democratic National Committee since 1980. She has worked actively for a variety of Democratic presidential candidates—African-American Jesse Jackson in 1984, liberal Edward Kennedy in 1980, and centrist Bill Clinton in 1992—seconding their nominations at national conventions and serving as cochair of their campaigns.

She became nationally renowned during the April 1992 riots that destroyed large parts of her own congressional district. Waters came home, saw the results of the rioting, and recognized it as an expression of the hopelessness and despair that so many disadvantaged city-dwellers felt. The way to prevent the rioting, she said, was to deal with the people's despair by providing schools and jobs in neglected city neighborhoods. When people spoke to her about white people's fear of violence, she told them about black people's fear of never escaping poverty.

Her own legislative office had burned to the ground during the disturbances, but she shrugged that off. Working from a temporary office in an airport coffee shop, she quickly made appointments with McDonald's and other large corporations, urging them to rebuild in the devastated area.

She walked throughout her district without fear. She joined gang members in a dance called the Electric Slide. And she pointed out that women looting a store for diapers

My life has to be about optimism. I can never believe that nothing can be done. . . . I have to believe that not only can we change things, but that I can contribute to that.

—Maxine Waters

Waters (center) with two Oakland, California, school officials before they testify at a Senate committee hearing on Ebonics, an African-American variation of English (AP/Wide World Photos)

would probably receive longer jail sentences than executives who looted their own savings and loans (a scandal at the time).

Following the riots, she founded Community Build, a grass-roots rebuilding project. Several of her bills provided similar chances to cities nationwide. Her Emergency Development Loan Guarantee Program, which became law in 1992, authorized $2 billion a year to cities for small business expansion and other economic development. Her 1993 Youth Fair Chance program has helped unemployed young people learn job and life skills.

Waters has worked actively to support the rights of people in several countries. She worked with the African National Congress to end apartheid and was part of the official U.S. delegation to Nelson Mandela's inauguration as the first democratically elected president of South Africa. She was arrested in front of the White House while urging justice for refugees from Haiti and the restoration of democracy in that Caribbean nation.

Even her most extreme comments are based on the reality of many people's lives in her district. She called President George Bush a "racist" and "mean-spirited," with "no care or concern" about African Americans. In 1997, she called for a government investigation into suggestions that the Central Intelligence Agency (CIA) was linked to sales of crack cocaine, which is popular among poor drug-users.

Since 1997, with a Republican majority in Congress, Waters has had a slightly lower profile. But, she has continued to support affirmative action for women and minority citizens and efforts to improve the education of African Americans. She was prominent in the 1997 Million Woman March in Philadelphia. As one of the keynote speakers, she called for strong government action to break up drug cartels and keep drugs out of the inner cities. Also, she joined several women's groups in seeking better pay for workers in developing nations' factories that produce sports shoes endorsed by high-profile women athletes.

In her own community of Watts, Waters has helped establish the Maxine Waters Employment Preparation Center. It provides education and employment opportunities for residents.

Chronology

AUGUST 15, 1938	Maxine Carr is born, St. Louis, Missouri
1940	Her parents separate; she and her mother move to a series of housing projects
1951	works as a bus girl, in a whites-only restaurant
1956–60	graduates from high school; marries Edward Waters; has two children, Edward and Karen

1961	the Waterses move to Los Angeles and settle in the Watts neighborhood; Maxine Waters begins work in a garment factory
1966	works as an assistant teacher in the federally-funded Head Start program for low-income preschoolers; is promoted to supervisor
1972	divorces Edward Waters
1973	manages David Cunningham's successful campaign for Los Angeles City Council; Cunningham names her his chief assistant
1976	is elected to California state assembly
1977	marries Sidney Williams, a former football player and an automobile salesman
1978–88	is reelected to the California state assembly
1980–PRESENT	serves as member of Democratic National Committee
1980	seconds Senator Edward Kennedy's nomination for president at Democratic National Convention
1984	serves as national cochair for Jesse Jackson's presidential campaign; seconds his nomination at Democratic National Convention
1990	is elected to U.S. House of Representatives
1992	speaks out about the frustrations and hopelessness of the disadvantaged rioters during the Los Angeles riots
1992	seconds Bill Clinton's presidential nomination at Democratic National Convention; serves as national cochair of his campaign

| 1992, 1994, 1996 | is re-elected to the U.S. House of Representatives |
| 1996 | is named chairperson of the Congressional Black Caucus |

Further Reading

Holmes, Steven A. "Call for C.I.A.-Cocaine Inquiry Is Renewed." *New York Times,* May 15, 1997, p. A17. Explanation of the story of a connection between the CIA and drug sales in African-American communities.

Janofsky, Michael. "At Million Women March, Focus Is on Family." *New York Times,* October 26, 1997, p. A1. Description of the march, including some of Waters's speech.

"Maxine Waters." *Current Biography Yearbook.* Bronx, N.Y.: H.W. Wilson, 1992. Sketch of the early part of Waters's life and career.

Smuit, Douglas. "Waters Focuses Her Rage at System." *Los Angeles Times,* May 10, 1992, p. 1. A comprehensive summary of Waters's actions during the Los Angeles Riots.

The following web page provides biographical material:

http://www.house.gov/waters/bio.htm

Patricia Scott Schroeder

(1940–)

Throughout the summer of 1987, Representative Patricia Scott Schroeder explored the idea of running for president. Her 15 years of political experience, however, told her she didn't have the time, the money, or the organization to put a professional campaign together. Home again in Denver, she announced her decision to a crowd of supporters.

When they started shouting "Run, Pat, run," she realized how much she'd wanted to run for president. She lost her usual reserved expression and began to cry. It was her tears, not her speech, that made news headlines. At first, some columnists thought that her tears killed women's presidential hopes for decades to come.

Then she started collecting and making public stories about tears shed by male politicians at similar moments—stories that hadn't made the news at the time. A former cabinet officer cried while giving his farewell speech. President Lyndon B. Johnson cried at a White House civil rights ceremony. Even George Washington cried at his farewell dinner with his Revolutionary War officers in 1783.

Representative Patricia Scott Schroeder in her House office during her first term, 1974
(AP/Wide World Photos)

All of a sudden, politicians, male and female, realized tears were a way of connecting with voters. Tears became a campaign tool, not a sign of weakness.

Patricia Nell Scott was born on July 30, 1940, in Portland, Oregon, the daughter of two native Nebraskans. Her father, Lee Scott, was in the aviation insurance business; her mother, Bernice Scott Scott, was a public school teacher. The family, including Patricia's brother Mike, moved frequently during her childhood. By the time they arrived in Des Moines, Iowa, where Patricia attended high school, the family had also lived in Texas, Missouri, Nebraska, and Ohio.

Both parents believed in one's independence and encouraged Patricia to be fearless and creative. She learned to fly an airplane when she was 15 and earned a pilot's license at age 16. She and her brother invented imaginative ways to earn money, including buying damaged and repairable merchandise, fixing it up, and selling it for a profit.

Lee Scott came from a family of Prairie Populists—part of a social, political, and economic movement that stressed equality and justice for all. His maternal grandmother had traveled west in a covered wagon from Massachusetts. His father's family came from Ireland during the 1860s, settled in Nebraska, and homesteaded a farm. In the 1880s, his father was elected to the Nebraska legislature, supporting the rights of farmers and laborers against industrialists and bankers. Patricia Schroeder claims her Populist heritage and feels comfortable as part of it.

After graduating from public high school in Des Moines in 1958, she attended the University of Minnesota. In three years, she graduated magna cum laude and was elected to Phi Beta Kappa. She next attended Harvard Law School, where she had her first experience with open sexism. Women had only recently been allowed to enroll in Harvard's law school. One male student seated next to her announced during class that he was going to ask for another seat because he refused to sit next to a woman.

In 1962, she married a fellow Harvard law student, James White Schroeder, a

> **M**ake the most of opportunities as they come up.
>
> —Patricia Scott Schroeder

midwesterner. He had told her that the only thing he didn't want in marriage was for it to be boring.

She received her J.D. degree in 1964. Following their graduation from law school, Patricia and Jim Schroeder settled in Denver. For several years, Schroeder worked full time as an attorney for the National Labor Relations Board, a government agency. She resigned when she became pregnant with their first child because the board didn't allow pregnant women to continue to work there. Their son Scott was born in 1966 and their daughter Jamie, in 1970.

While taking care of her small children, Schroeder also worked at several part-time jobs. She lectured in law and worked as a hearing officer for the Colorado Personnel Department. She also acted as an unpaid lawyer for the local chapter of Planned Parenthood—a nationwide family planning organization.

In 1972, Patricia Schroeder entered elective politics almost by accident. The Democrats in her district had a disastrous loss in the 1970 congressional race. In 1972, no male politician wanted to run for the seat since the Democrats were expected to lose once again. Jim Schroeder, who was active in the Young Democrats, was asked by another member if his wife would be willing to run. No woman had ever been elected to Congress from Colorado, so she would be a different kind of candidate.

With her husband as campaign manager, Schroeder accepted the offer. The Democratic National Committee turned down their request for campaign funds, so they organized a grassroots campaign. She campaigned on current issues—opposing the Vietnam War and supporting environmental protection.

She was sure she would lose, so she kept working at her regular jobs throughout the whole campaign. To everyone's surprise, she won with 52 percent of the vote in a year when the Republican presidential candidate, Richard Nixon, won by a large majority. Schroeder was reelected 11 times and never faced serious opposition.

Even before she arrived in Washington, many news reporters and fellow congressmembers saw Schroeder as a different kind of congress-woman. She was young, just 32, and the only congresswoman with young children. Her husband was willing to relocate his law practice to Washington. As she says, she was the only House member who came on the floor with diapers in her handbag, the only one with a bowl of crayons on her office coffee table, and the only one to give a birthday party for kindergartners in the House members' dining room.

Schroeder entered Congress at the beginning of a social revolution. The women's movement was gaining strength and "women's issues" became politically important. These issues included child care, parental leave, pension reform for stay-at-home wives and former wives, and taxation.

These issues remained important to her throughout her congressional career. For instance, the nation's first comprehensive bill for a governmental role in child care was passed in Congress in 1971 but vetoed by the president. For the next 15 years, Schroeder was a leader in the struggle to have such a bill passed and signed into law.

She was a feminist before entering politics and remained one. Feminist leader Gloria Steinem had helped raise funds for her first campaign.

Schroeder also wanted to change the social priorities expressed in the federal budget, especially by spending less on the military and more on social values. She decided that the best way to do this was to be appointed to the Armed Services Committee. It approved the military budget, but it also had the most discretionary funds—money the Committee could distribute in the budget as it wanted to. The committee was all male, the official reason for this being that women had no combat experience. Schroeder, though, discovered that several male committee members hadn't been in combat, either. Finally, she was named to the committee.

As an example of her priorities, she wanted to reduce waste in the purchase of military equipment and use the extra money for family issues. Generals told her privately that child care was important to them. Enlisted men and women often mentioned inadequate child care as a reason not to reenlist. But they felt that they couldn't ask for child care funds because they didn't want to seem "soft." Her response: The military won't make child care a higher priority until it's all right for men to support these and other family issues.

As a committee member she also championed numerous issues related to women in the military, including more medical research on women's health at military hospitals and the availability of abortions in foreign countries. The military didn't always have these priorities, and she was often ridiculed for her efforts. She was

> I *have a uterus and a brain and they both work.*
>
> —Patricia Scott Schroeder

particularly outspoken about sexual harassment in the military. One such episode was during the Tailhook convention in 1991 in which male naval officers were later reprimanded or demoted for harassing or assaulting women officers and enlisted sailors.

Many of these issues carried over into civilian life, and she continued to work on them in other committees of Congress. During her career, she was also a member of the House Select Committee on Children, Youth, and Families; the Judiciary Committee; and the Post Office and Civil Service Committee, chairing the Subcommittee on Civil Service. And she cochaired the House Armed Services Task Force on Defense Burden Sharing, which looked for ways to share our defense costs with our allies. She was a leader in convincing the National Institutes of Health (NIH) to include women as well as men in long-term health studies. She also encouraged the NIH to expand its studies of women's diseases, such as ovarian cancer.

Schroeder believes that her special closeness to family issues comes from a difficult experience in her own childhood and from problems she had bearing her own children. An eye condition forced her to wear glasses when she was a baby. She wore a patch over one eye for several years, making her "different" from others in her classroom. Sometimes other children made fun of her.

When she was pregnant with Scott, she was overcome by carbon monoxide gas in her home. She was fearful that he would develop abnormally. Fortunately this didn't happen. Two years later, she had an abnormal pregnancy with unusual bleeding. At first, the doctors told her that the bleeding was caused by her unsuccessful adjustment to being a housewife. Then, it was discovered that one of the twins she was carrying had died in the womb. The other twin died of a brain hemorrhage shortly after birth. After an uneventful pregnancy with Jamie, she began to hemorrhage so severely that she spent six weeks, including her 30th birthday, in intensive care. She was told that another pregnancy would kill her.

These experiences made her believe even more strongly that a woman should have control over her own body. In 1962, when she married in Massachusetts, state law made it illegal to sell contraceptives even to married couples. Not until three years later did the Supreme Court give married couples access to contraceptives nationwide.

Roe v. *Wade,* the legal case in which the Supreme Court allowed abortions, occurred in 1973, three years after her final pregnancy. Since then, many women have felt forced to choose between being "pro life" or "pro choice." Schroeder considers herself both, because of her problem pregnancies.

Among the pregnancy-related issues she has championed are better birth control information for teens, health insurance that covers infertility testing and treatment, and insurance that covers the costs of adoption. In 1977, she was a sponsor of the Pregnancy Discrimination Act, which amended the Civil Rights Act in order to keep women from being fired if they became pregnant.

Schroeder set up a flextime program in the federal government, allowing workers to begin and end work days at times they determine, rather than on a set schedule. This makes it easier to schedule, for instance, medical appointments and school conferences. The program was later adopted by many government agencies. She also helped create career-oriented part-time jobs in the federal government. Her legislation also provided before- and after-school care programs.

In 1984, she sponsored the Retirement Equity Act, which when it became law, gave pensions to divorced wives of some federal workers. This aided women who were expected to do unpaid work for their diplomat-husbands in the State Department's Foreign Service.

Schroeder also strongly supported the Family and Medical Leave Act, which provided unpaid leave from jobs for people to care for newborn babies, newly-adopted children, and serious family illness. The bill passed in Congress several times but was vetoed by President George Bush. In 1993, the bill was given top priority. It passed and was signed by President Bill Clinton.

For many years Schroeder was a cochair of the Women's Issues Caucus, a congressional group of women and men who supported bills important to women. Many of these were enacted, such as the Violence Against Women Act of 1990. This law doubles the penalty set forth in federal sentencing guidelines for repeat offenders of sexual abuse, aggravated sexual abuse, or abusive sexual contact. It also provides grants to local governments for training of police, judges, and court personnel to prevent violent crimes against women, as well as rape prevention education. It changes rules of evidence to prevent embarrassment of victims on the witness stand and to prevent introduction of a victim's previous sexual behavior in a current case. The law also requires payment of restitution by a convicted defendant for income lost, attorneys' fees, and costs of obtaining protection orders. And, it encourages arrest of an abusive spouse and provides funding for shelters. It also asserts that victims have the right to be free from discrimination on the basis of gender in the street and at home, as well as in the workplace (which was protected under previous laws).

Also, she helped pass the Gender Equity in Education Act, which required schools receiving federal funds to spend equally for women and men, and the Freedom of Access to Clinic Entrances Act, which protected women entering clinics for abortions or other treatment. The Caucus also promoted women's health in defense-related businesses and in veterans' hospitals.

Schroeder (pointing) and other congresswomen march to the Senate floor in 1994 to support women senators during a vote. (AP/Wide World Photos)

During her long congressional career, Schroeder never became an "insider"—one of those in the House's power structure. Her party leaders thought she wasn't a reliable team player. She felt that, as a woman, she could never be part of the leadership. Instead, she made her reputation nationally as an independent. This stance also worked well in her home district. As she was elected term after term, her seniority in the House increased, giving her some of the leadership status that insiders also had.

She always spoke up for the issues she championed, whether the leadership approved or not. She often dramatized women's concerns, several times leading groups of congresswomen onto the Senate floor to support bills being debated there.

In 1996, Schroeder decided not to seek reelection. She taught at Princeton University's Woodrow Wilson School of Government in the first part of 1997. Later that year, she was named president of the Association of American Publishers, a trade organization, whose head-quarters is in Washington, D.C.

Chronology

JULY 30, 1940	Patricia Scott is born, Portland, Oregon
1961	graduates from University of Minnesota; enters Harvard Law School
1962	marries James Schroeder, a fellow law student
1964	receives J.D. from Harvard Law School
1964	works as field attorney for the National Labor Relations Board
1966–70	has two children: Scott and Jamie
1969	works as law lecturer and instructor at the Community College of Denver; University of Colorado, Denver; and Regis College

1971	works as hearing officer for the Colorado Personnel Department
1972	is elected to U.S. House of Representatives
1974–94	is reelected to U.S. House of Representatives
1984	Cochairs Representative Gary Hart's presidential campaign
1987	explores possibility of running for president; decides not to run
1995	announces her retirement from Congress at the end of her term
1997	is named president of the Association of American Publishers

Further Reading

Bingham, Clara. *Women On the Hill: Challenging the Culture of Congress.* New York: Times Books/Random House, 1997. This is an entertaining description of the way Schroeder and three other Congressional women worked together on selected issues. It provides a behind-the-scenes look at the way Congress works.

Schroeder, Pat. *24 Years of House Work and the Place Is Still a Mess.* Kansas City, Mo.: Andrews & McMeel, 1998. The book includes stories and reflections on her career.

Schroeder, Pat, with Andrea Camp and Robyn Lipner. *Champion of the Great American Family.* New York: Random House, 1989. Schroeder's autobiography emphasizes her political career, but with much personal background.

The following web pages provide biographical and background material about Schroeder:

http://www.publishers.org/news/releases/former.html
http://www.vote-smart.org

Christine Todd Whitman

(1946–)

Did she really want to be a Republican? Her parents were active in the Republican party. But that reason wasn't good enough. Also, all her friends were Democrats. She thought about it, then finally decided. She believed that if you treated everyone with dignity and gave them the chance to make their own life decisions, you showed them more respect than if you put them in large government programs. That was the Republican way and she chose to be a Republican.

She was Christine Todd, and she was 13 years old.

Christine Temple Todd was born into a wealthy family in rural New Jersey on September 26, 1946, the youngest of four children. Her parents, Webster and Eleanor Schley Todd, were both active in New Jersey Republican politics. In fact, they met at the 1932 Republican National Convention.

New Jersey governor Christine Todd Whitman in 1995 announcing that she is not interested in being considered for the Republican vice presidential nomination (AP/Wide World Photos)

Her father came from a long line of Presbyterian ministers in the East and the Midwest. Webster Todd and his father were partners in a construction business in New York. Through an acquaintanceship with John D. Rockefeller Sr., the Todds were chosen to build Rockefeller Center in New York City and to restore Colonial Williamsburg in Virginia.

Webster Todd was chairman of the New Jersey Republican party from 1964 to 1969 and from 1974 to 1977. Both Christine Todd's grandfathers, John Todd and Reeve Schley, a banker, had been finance chairmen of the New Jersey Republican party.

Eleanor Schley Todd came from a wealthy and well-connected family of politically active women. She was a national vice-chairperson of the Republican party. Before that, she succeeded her own mother, Kate Prentice Schley, as Republican national committeewoman in New Jersey.

Both families settled in "horse country" New Jersey near the beginning of the 20th century and lived in an aristocratic style. When Webster and Eleanor Todd were married in 1933, the Schley's gave the couple a working farm and estate named Pontefract after the village in England that the Todds had emigrated from in the early 1600s.

Christine—called Christie since childhood—grew up at Pontefract. After her parents died, she and her husband, John Whitman, moved there, and still live there today. In the Todd family, it was expected that Christine would love the farm, ride horses, and attend private schools. She learned to ride before she went to kindergarten and rode in horseshows during her teens.

Christine was an indifferent student, receiving a conditional eighth grade diploma from Far Hills Country Day School because she flunked Latin. Her parents attempted to send her to Foxcroft, a boarding high school in Virginia that her mother and older sister had attended, but she stayed only one year because she was too homesick. She graduated in 1964 from the Chapin School, in New York City, where she was an average student, played softball and field hockey, and formed a current events club. Her senior year, she ran a mock Republican convention, which nominated her favorite candidate, New York governor Nelson Rockefeller.

In the summer of 1964, she was honored at a dinner dance given by her grandparents—the equivalent of a debutante's coming-out party. One of the guests, the date of another young woman, was John Whitman. He was a Yale University student, the son of a judge, and the grandson of a former New York governor. During the next 10 years they saw each other occasionally in Washington and in New Jersey and finally married in 1974.

Christine Todd graduated from Wheaton College, in Norton, Massachusetts—then a women's college—in 1968 with an honors degree in government. Her senior thesis was on Nigeria's democracy.

During her college years, she was an activist. She demonstrated in favor of birth control; tried smoking pot (she *did* inhale); worked in the Young Republicans, serving as president her senior year; and was vice president of her senior class. She invited prominent progressive Republicans, such as Senator Edward Brooke of Massachusetts and Tom Kean, who was later the governor of New Jersey, to come and speak. She even invited drug guru Timothy Leary to speak under Young Republican auspices—to stimulate discussion, she said—but he didn't come.

During her freshman year, she attended the Young Republican National Leadership Training School in Washington, D.C. She hoped to help the largely conservative party attract new and diverse leadership in the future.

Because of her political background, she grew up with the confidence to plan and achieve these goals. Her parents always found ways to involve her in their political activities. Through them, she met prominent politicians and three future presidents. Her parents also encouraged Dwight Eisenhower to seek the presidency, even by following him to Paris (where he held a NATO position) to urge him to run. In a well-publicized event, young Christine presented presidential candidate Eisenhower with a golf tee holder. After Eisenhower was elected, he appointed Webster Todd to a NATO post in Paris, where Christine and her mother accompanied him.

Richard Nixon's two daughters had been her schoolmates at the Chapin School. George Bush and his wife Barbara were family friends. Future New Jersey governor Tom Kean, another political ally of her father, appointed her to her first statewide post.

Whitman has always been allied with the Republican party's moderate wing. Her first paying job after graduation in 1968 was in Nelson Rockefeller's unsuccessful presidential campaign in which he lost the nomination to Richard Nixon. After Nixon was elected president, Christine worked first as a special assistant to the director of the U.S. Office of Economic Opportunity and then for the Republican National Committee (RNC), the party's governing and policy-making group.

Soon realizing that the Republican political world was strongly male-oriented, she developed the idea for a new job combining travel and research and presented it to the RNC. With the committee's go-ahead, she spent a year touring the country and meeting with diverse groups. They included college radicals, inner-city gang members, senior citizens, women, and other people not usually addressed by Republican party strategy. At the end of the year, she wrote a report on her findings, describing how the party could reach out to these groups.

Later, she worked in the Peace Corps's Washington office. Along with her brother Dan, in 1972 she worked for the Committee to Reelect the President (Nixon) and after his victory, on his transition team.

In 1974, she and John Whitman married, after agreeing on a life plan. In the first years, he would work hard at his job as an investment banker and she would be primarily a wife and mother. When the children were older, he would take greater responsibility for them, while she pursued a full-time political life. (Their children are Kate, born in 1977, and Taylor, born in 1979.)

Even during the early years of their marriage, Christine Whitman kept in touch with politics. When John was transferred to London, England, for two years, Whitman was unable to work because of the restrictions on John's visa. Instead, she became the representative of Republicans Abroad, an organization of Republicans living in Europe.

Once in New Jersey again, she served part time on a local water district board and on the board of the local community college district. In 1980, Eleanor Todd, her mother, was chairperson of the finance committee for George Bush's New Jersey presidential campaign. Christine Whitman was cochairperson.

CHRISTINE TODD WHITMAN

She finally plunged into full-time elective politics in 1982 when she was elected as a Chosen Freeholder of her county (the equivalent of a county supervisor). Much of Whitman's time on the board involved waste management, such as landfill siting and waste recycling. Developing sites and priorities to meet the needs of the county's commercial developments, inner-city areas, and chicken farms, as well as expensive estates, was a challenge and a testing ground for a first-time official.

In 1988, Governor Tom Kean nominated Whitman to the Board of Public Utilities, which regulates the rates that utility companies charge. With Kean's approval, she was elected the board's president, with a seat in the governor's cabinet. By 1990, she was looking ahead to other political positions.

In 1990, she volunteered to run as the Republican senatorial candidate against Senator Bill Bradley, who was considered unbeatable. By doing this, it was the unspoken agreement that the party would support her in a future election for an office she could win.

Whitman found Bradley vulnerable on the subject of state taxes. Bradley's strategy was to ignore the topic because it was a state issue, not a federal one, but his strategy only made him look distant and out of touch with his voters' concerns. Whitman hammered away at the subject and gained support.

She was expected to lose by 16–32 percentage points. Instead, she lost by just two points. Even though she lost, she became known nationally as a Republican "star."

Almost immediately, she started running for governor. She formed a committee to raise money and started meeting with Republican voters statewide. Again, the topic was taxes. This time, the subject under attack was the large tax increase put into effect by Governor James Florio, a Democrat. Like Bradley, Florio was considered unbeatable. But Whitman surprised politicians and voters alike by announcing a plan to cut taxes by 30 percent if she became governor—a promise most voters refused to believe.

Her major disadvantage was her background of wealth and privilege. There also were controversies from her previous offices. She voted to raise her own salary as a Chosen Freeholder. A "blind trust" that she set up to manage her investments while in office, was handled by her family's bank, where she herself was on the board of directors. She also voted to put county money in that same bank. As Board of Public Utilities president, she was accused of allowing the development of land that was supposed to stay in its natural form—an action that was overturned in court. She claimed that she followed state procedures in making the decision.

Despite these problems, she defeated her nearest primary opponent by seven points.

In the general election campaign, she was accused of classifying Pontefract as a farm rather than as an estate in order to pay lower property taxes. She fought back strongly on this, inviting the press to a cookout and a tour of the fields, barns, and animals. When a news crew threatened to fly over the land and count the animals, the Whitmans painted a huge sign on the barn roof stating the amount of taxes they paid.

She was able to put the "rich folks" image aside with her outgoing campaign style; a good performance in a debate with Florio, which was televised statewide; and her focus on Florio's tax increase.

The polls always showed her running behind him, but on election night, she defeated Florio by one percentage point. Her victory was a combination of her winning the Republican areas by a wide margin and taking Democratic voters away from Florio with her tax reduction plan.

What should have been a great celebration suddenly turned into a nightmare. Her campaign manager, Ed Rollins, was a well-known Republican political consultant. A week after the election, Rollins told a press breakfast in Washington, D.C., that Whitman's successful strategy had been to spend $500,000 on two projects: as campaign-contributed funds to African-American churches that agreed not to endorse Governor Florio and as payments to Democratic workers to stay home on election day.

> I'm not interested in being governor of New Jersey. I am interested in governing New Jersey.
>
> —Christine Todd Whitman

Whitman immediately condemned Rollins's claim. "It did not happen," she said. "It's not only illegal, it's immoral, and I do not play the game that way."

Jesse Jackson and other African-American leaders were outraged and threatened to march on her headquarters in protest. The FBI and the state election law enforcement commission immediately began investigations. The next day, Rollins retracted his statement. No wrongdoing was uncovered. The verdict: Rollins's statement was a total lie.

Whitman was sworn in as governor on January 18, 1994, as New Jersey's first woman governor. She used the same Bible that had been used 79 years earlier when her husband's grandfather, Charles S. Whitman Sr., was sworn in as governor of New York.

In her first term, her four priorities were the economy, education, cities, and juvenile justice. Despite the voters' skepticism, she announced the first 5 percent tax reduction in her inaugural address. She completed the full 30 percent reduction in 1995, a year ahead

Whitman greets traders on the floor of the New York Stock Exchange, in 1995. (AP/Wide World Photos)

Whitman and Republican presidential candidate Bob Dole marching in a Columbus Day parade in 1996 (AP/Wide World Photos)

CHRISTINE TODD WHITMAN

of schedule. Since the Whitmans are in a very high tax bracket, they pledged to contribute the difference between their taxes under the old rate and under the reduced rate to charity.

One of the factors that made her 30 percent tax reduction promise a possibility was the great power the state of New Jersey's governor holds. As governor, Whitman can make line-item vetoes—a power she used to control state spending. She can make a conditional veto. This lets her rewrite a bill that's been passed by the legislature and send it back to be voted up or down as she's rewritten it. As the only elected statewide officeholder, she also appoints all the other major officeholders in the state government (the attorney general, secretary of state, supreme court, and all state judges), with the advice and consent of the state senate. In most other states these offices are elective. (There is no lieutenant governor.)

In her first term, Whitman largely kept her election promises, but not without some setbacks. Lowering taxes lessened the amount of money available for state employees' pension funds. She made up the difference by issuing state bonds and using the proceeds to purchase stock for the pension funds. She has been criticized for this risky transaction. Also, she tried to meet federal school improvement requirements with educational standards rather than money. A court struck down her plan.

In 1997, she won her reelection primary race and campaigned for the general election, stressing the effectiveness of her economic program. The campaign's main issues were state property tax rates and the high cost of car insurance. Without the support of conservative Republicans who opposed her pro-choice position on abortion, she won by one percentage point over her main rival, Democrat James E. McGreevey. As a "lame duck"—an officeholder who cannot run for reelection—she is likely to be less effective in her second term than in her first.

> **P**eople better be a little careful of this lame duck. She's got four years to quack.
>
> —Christine Todd Whitman

Chronology

SEPTEMBER 26, 1946	Christine Temple Todd is born, Oldwick, New Jersey
1968	graduates from Wheaton College
1974	marries John Russell Whitman, an investment banker
1977–79	has two children: Kate and Taylor
1982–88	serves as a Chosen Freeholder of Somerset County, New Jersey
1988	appointed chairwoman of the New Jersey Public Utilities Board
1990	enters race for Senate against incumbent Bill Bradley; is defeated by a narrow margin
1993	is elected governor of New Jersey
1994	is sworn in as governor
1997	wins a narrow victory for a second term as governor

Further Reading

Aron, Michael. *Governor's Race: A TV Reporter's Chronicle of the 1993 Florio/Whitman Campaign.* New Brunswick, N.J.: Rutgers University Press, 1994. The book is a diarylike, day-by-day account of Whitman's campaign, as told by a political reporter for New Jersey Public Television.

Beard, Patricia. *Growing Up Republican: Christie Whitman: The Politics of Character.* New York: HarperCollins Publishers, 1996. This biography was written with Whitman's cooperation. More than a political biography, it provides colorful background material on Whitman's life and political priorities.

Lodop, Linda. *Political Leaders.* New York: Twenty-First Century Books, 1996.

McClure, Sandy. *Christie Whitman for the People: A Political Biography.* Amherst, N.Y.: Prometheus Books, 1996. This is another biography, written by a political reporter for a New Jersey newspaper. It concentrates on the campaign, but also includes some personal background.

Preston, Jennifer. "Whitman Pleased With Slim Victory in New Jersey." *New York Times,* November 6, 1997, p. A1. Overview and analysis of Whitman's reelection.

Carol
Moseley-Braun

(1947–)

I t was 1966 and the Reverend Martin Luther King Jr. was marching against racial discrimination in Chicago. Nineteen-year-old Carol Moseley was one of those marching with him. Opponents jeered from the sidelines, some of them throwing rocks. As Carol Moseley watched, a rock hit Dr. King, but he continued marching. She was deeply moved by his dignity in the face of violence that day.

She vowed to pursue racial equality by following King's nonviolent methods, even as she remembered how during her youth, she hid under her desk at her newly integrated grade school, while protesters threw rocks through the school windows. In school and in elected office, she worked against racism and for African-American equality, integrated environments, and greater participation by women. In 1992, she became the first African-American woman to be elected a U.S. senator.

Senator Carol Moseley-Braun in 1993 (AP/Wide World Photos)

Carol Elizabeth Moseley was born in Chicago on August 16, 1947. Her father, Joseph Moseley, was a policeman, and her mother, Edna Davie Moseley, was a medical technician. She was her parents' first child and was later joined by a sister and two brothers. Her first home was in an apartment building her family owned in a middle-class city neighborhood.

When Carol was a teenager, Joseph Moseley quit the police force and became a real estate salesman. He was also active in union and political activities. He took Carol to political meetings with him, where she learned that people can choose a government that helps create a more just society.

Despite these enriching periods, Carol's family life was troubled by her father's occasional violent outbursts, which sometimes turned into forms of physical child abuse, including beating Carol and her siblings. Carol sought refuge at her grandmother's house, but she also tried to bring the family back together peacefully.

When Carol was in her mid-teens, her parents divorced, and her mother moved the family to her grandmother's home in Oakwood, an impoverished part of Chicago's African-American ghetto. The new neighborhood was so violent that it was nicknamed the "Bucket of Blood." During her high school years, Carol worked part time in a grocery store to help her mother save enough money to move to a more peaceful neighborhood.

During these days, she also became a civil rights activist. She staged a "sit-in" at a lunch counter that refused to serve African Americans. When she was finally served the coffee that she ordered, she paid for it and left without drinking it. She had made her point.

She stood up against rock-throwers preventing racial integration of a Chicago beach. She volunteered in a school lunch program run by the Black Panthers, a radical "Black power" group, but refused to take part in their more confrontational activities.

Moseley graduated from the University of Illinois, Chicago, in 1969, with a B.A. in political science. She earned a J.D. in 1972 from the University of Chicago's law school, where she formed a Black Law Students Association.

CAROL MOSELEY-BRAUN

In 1973, she married a friend from law school, Michael Braun. Their son Matthew was born in 1976.

Carol Moseley-Braun's first job as a lawyer was as an assistant attorney in the U.S. Attorney's office in Chicago. Here she learned to work with Republicans as well as Democrats who were attracted to political life. For her work, Moseley-Braun earned the U.S. Attorney General's Special Achievement Award. From there, she joined a Chicago law firm. She was on her way to becoming a successful attorney but in 1978 decided instead to run for the state house of representatives.

She spent the next 10 years in that post, being reelected four times. She became recognized for her ability to build coalitions, particularly to pass laws for better education, racial equality in housing, and more efficient government. She also opposed the death penalty and worked for welfare reform. Every year she won a "best legislator" award from the Independent Voters of Illinois, a citizens' group.

In 1980, she became an assistant house majority leader, becoming the first African American and the first woman to hold that post in the state of Illinois. In 1983, Harold Washington, Chicago's first African-American mayor, chose her to be the legislative floor leader. This job made her responsible for getting Washington-sponsored bills passed by the state house of representatives. Despite her working relationship with Washington, he opposed her plan to run for lieutenant governor in 1986.

The year 1986 was a difficult time in Moseley-Braun's life. She and Michael Braun were divorced, her mother became seriously ill, and a brother and her father died. As she worked her way through these tragedies by focusing more intensely on her work, she decided to run for higher political office.

The next year, with Harold Washington's approval and help, she was elected recorder of deeds in Cook County, which includes Chicago. Again she was a trail-blazer, becoming the first African American and the first woman to hold an executive office in the county government. The office was widely thought of as old-fashioned and filled with corrupt practices. Moseley-Braun became well known for modernizing the office and for establishing its code of ethics.

Newly elected Senator Moseley-Braun thanking supporters in downtown Chicago, in 1992 (AP/Wide World Photos)

Her election as U.S. senator began with a seemingly unrelated incident in Washington, D.C. In 1991, President George Bush appointed a fellow Republican, Clarence Thomas, to the U.S. Supreme Court. In an extraordinary set of nomination hearings before the Senate Judiciary Committee, a law professor from Oklahoma, Anita Hill, accused Thomas of sexual harassment. Thomas and Hill were both African Americans. All the Senate committee members were white men. Like many women, Moseley-Braun thought Hill's testimony was convincing, but the committee and later the full Senate voted to confirm Thomas.

One of the people who voted "Yes" was a liberal Democrat from Illinois, Alan Dixon, who was running for reelection in 1992. Outraged, Moseley-Braun decided to enter the race herself.

Dixon had the support of the Democratic party in Illinois, so Moseley-Braun couldn't count on financial or organizational help. Instead, she ran a grassroots campaign for the Democratic nomination. With Kegosie Matthews, a former aide to the Reverend Jesse Jackson, as campaign manager, she won the nomination, defeating

Dixon and another candidate. She won the general election with 53 percent of the vote. This included 95 percent of the state's African-American vote, 58 percent of women's votes, and almost half of the white vote.

At the same time, some of her personal actions were viewed as controversial. She became personally involved with Matthews, who was unpopular with some campaign workers. After the election, two women who worked on the campaign accused him of sexual harassment, although this was never proven. Moseley-Braun was accused of improperly keeping money that should have been paid to Medicare during her mother's illness. Many of these same charges reappeared in 1997, as she campaigned for reelection.

The day after she was sworn in, Moseley-Braun was one of two women senators appointed to the Judiciary Committee. In 1998, she served on the Banking, Housing, and Urban Affairs Committee and the Special Committee on Aging. She has also served on the Small

Moseley-Braun, at a 1994 news conference, endorses Chicago mayor Richard M. Daley for reelection. (AP/Wide World Photos)

Business Committee and the Bi-partisan Commission on Entitlements and Tax Reform.

In May 1993, she used her unique position as the only African-American senator to raise the consciousness of her colleagues. The subject was a seemingly routine but obscure vote on a design patent. She took the lead in the Judiciary Committee to defeat a bill to extend a design patent for the emblem of the United Daughters of the Confederacy, an organization composed of descendants of Confederate soldiers. She objected to official recognition of this emblem because it contained the flag of the Confederate States of America.

In July, the bill was reintroduced on the Senate floor as an amendment to a national service bill. She spoke briefly in opposition. "[W]e are duty bound," she said, "to honor our ancestors . . . by asking whether such recognition by the U.S. Senate is appropriate." Even though it was over 100 years since the Confederacy ended, she said, "the emblems of the Confederacy have meaning to Americans." She urged the Senate to vote "No," but the bill passed, 52:48.

She rose and spoke again, this time more passionately. The vote, she said, "is about race." She said that she "had been stunned about how often and how much race comes up in [Senate] debate." She continued, "The issue is whether or not Americans, such as myself, . . . will have to suffer the indignity of being reminded time and time again, that at one point in this country's history we were human chattel. We were property. We could be traded, bought, and sold." She continued, "It is an outrage. It is an insult. It is absolutely unacceptable to me and to millions of Americans, black or white, that we would put the imprimatur of the United States Senate on a symbol of this kind of idea."

I would like to put a stake through the heart of this particular Dracula [the patent for the United Daughters of the Confederacy emblem] and hope it never comes up again.

—Carol Moseley-Braun

In response, senator after senator rose to say that she was right, that they had not realized the symbolism in the original vote. The Senate voted again. This time, it defeated the patent extension, 75:25.

Moseley-Braun can be equally passionate about issues that are important to women of all races. She is a member of the League of Women Voters and is proud of the struggle that won women the right to vote in 1920. In 1996, she spoke out to preserve the rights of women to have abortions if necessary, even the "partial birth abortion," a controversial late-term procedure.

The first bill she introduced and passed required Congress to disclose the costs of unfunded mandates (federal requirements that the states must pay for). Among the education-related bills she has supported is the Education Infrastructure Act, which provides funds to repair schools and libraries. She has also coordinated a public/private partnership in Chicago that allows school children to use computer equipment donated by private companies. She also introduced and helped pass a bill that makes it easier for custodial parents to obtain child support payments.

She was the author of the "brownfields" provision in the balanced budget bill passed in 1997. Brownfields are abandoned, lightly-contaminated industrial and commercial sites, usually in the inner city. The bill provided a tax incentive for businesses to buy them, to clean them up, and then to open them for use.

She also introduced a bill that provides procedures for handling sexual or racial harassment in the Armed Forces. It eventually became law. She cosponsored the Community Development Financial Institutions Act, which gives people and businesses in underserved neighborhoods improved access to bank funds. Another law sets goals for federal contracts for small, women-owned businesses.

Reproductive choice is, in the final analysis, about the relationship of women citizens, of female citizens to their Government. Reproductive choice is central to their liberty.

—Carol Moseley-Braun

Moseley-Braun greets well-wishers at the Democratic National Convention in Chicago, 1996. (AP/Wide World Photos)

She introduced the Women's Pension Equity Act of 1996, to allow wives and former wives fair amounts of the pensions their husbands earned during the marriage. Several sections were enacted as parts of other laws.

She was active in amending and passing the Violent Crime Control and Law Enforcement Act of 1994. This law offers alternatives to communities to prevent crime before one is committed.

In 1997, she began running for reelection in 1998 and soon was criticized for another personal decision. In 1996, during a visit to Africa, she met secretly with Nigeria's dictator—an action that drew criticism from the State Department for lending legitimacy to his repressive regime. Also drawing criticism was the fact that she was accompanied by Kegosie Matthews, who is now a registered agent of the Nigerian government.

Moseley-Braun says the trip combined a vacation and an attempt at personal diplomacy.

CAROL MOSELEY-BRAUN

Voters will decide in 1998 whether her legislative skill can overcome her personal difficulties.

Chronology

AUGUST 16, 1947	Carole Elizabeth Moseley is born, in Chicago, Illinois
1969	graduates from University of Illinois, Chicago, with a B.A. in political science
1972	graduates with a J.D. from University of Chicago law school
1973	marries Michael Braun, a friend from law school
1976	gives birth to son Matthew
1978	is elected to the state house of representatives
1986	divorces Michael Braun
1987	is elected Cook County recorder of deeds
1992–PRESENT	serves as a U.S. senator

Further Reading

Berke, Richard L. "Democrats Hitch Hopes to a Not-So-Shining Star." *New York Times,* July 4, 1997, p. A1. Analysis of Moseley-Braun's political situation at the start of her reelection campaign.

Congressional Record, July 22, 1993, p. S9251. Debate and votes, including Moseley-Braun's remarks, on the United Daughters of the Confederacy design patent extension.

Huggins, Nathan. I., ed. *Carol Moseley-Braun: Politician.* New York: Chelsea House Publishers, 1995.

Morin, Isobel V. *Women of the U.S. Congress.* Minneapolis, Minn.: Oliver Press, Inc., 1994.

"Moseley-Braun, Carol." *Current Biography Yearbook.* Bronx, N.Y.: H. W. Wilson, 1994. Sketch of Moseley-Braun's life and career.

Pollack, Jill S. *Women on the Hill: A History of Women in Congress.* Danbury, Conn.: Franklin Watts, 1996.

The following web pages provide biographical material:

http://www.senate.gov/member/il/moseley-braun/general
http://www.vote-smart.org

Ileana Ros-Lehtinen

(1952–   )

Ileana Ros was seven years old when she and her parents left the Communist repression in their native Cuba, a Caribbean nation. They settled in Miami, Florida, where Ileana, who spoke only Spanish, began school. At that early age, she made several promises to herself. She would learn English; she would become an American citizen; and she would be helpful to others who also came to this country from Cuba. She might even serve in the United States government.

In 1972, Ileana became a U.S. citizen. In 1989, she became the first Cuban American and the first Hispanic woman elected to the U.S. House of Representatives.

★★★

Ileana Ros was born on July 15, 1952, in Havana, Cuba's capital and its largest city. Her parents, Enrique Emilio Ros, an accountant, and Amanda Adato Ros, disliked the limitations of personal freedom placed on Cubans by Fidel Castro's Marxist government, which came to power in 1959. In 1960, they brought their two children to Miami, a city in nearby southern Florida that was becoming a gathering place for anti-Castro Cubans.

At first, the Ros family thought of themselves as refugees and planned to return to Cuba one day. After the failure of a U.S.-backed

Representative Ileana Ros-Lehtinen answers questions from the audience. (Courtesy Rep. Ileana Ros-Lehtinen)

ILEANA ROS-LEHTINEN

> I *was a little refugee girl . . . bewildered when I entered the classroom for the first time. But America wrapped her arms around me. . . . embraced me and gave me heart.*
>
> —Ileana Ros-Lehtinen

invasion at Cuba's Bay of Pigs in 1961, they changed their minds. They decided they would stay in the United States for many years and wanted their children to become Americans.

After completing high school, Ileana Ros earned an Associate of Arts degree, in 1972, from Miami Dade Community College. That same year, she became a U.S. citizen. She then earned a B.A. with honors in English (1975) and an M.S. with honors in educational leadership (1987) from Florida International University. In 1997, she was working toward a doctorate in educational administration at the University of Miami.

During the 1970s she founded the Eastern Academy, a bilingual private school in the Miami area. She was its principal for 10 years.

A Republican, Ros began her political career in 1982, when she became the first Hispanic woman elected to the Florida house of representatives. She served through 1986 and then was elected to the state senate from 1986 until 1989, becoming the first Hispanic woman in that house as well. During this period, she helped prevent oil drilling in the wilderness area called the Everglades. She also supported environmental restoration of the Miami River. She played a leading role in passing a Victim's Bill of Rights for the state constitution. Legislation that benefits young people was also high on her agenda, and she introduced both a prepaid college tuition program and a missing children's identification program.

In the Florida house of representatives, she met a fellow legislator, Dexter Lehtinen, whom she later married. They became the only married couple in any of the state legislatures. Dexter Lehtinen later became the U.S. attorney for Miami. They have two children, Amanda (born in 1986) and Patricia (born in 1988). Ros-Lehtinen also has two stepchildren.

Ros-Lehtinen campaigning in 1989 in Little Havana Senior Center (Miami) for a seat in Congress (AP/Wide World Photos)

> *The America*
> *I know is caring . . .*
> *inclusive . . .*
> *nurturing . . .*
> *encouraging.*
> *The America I know*
> *brims with opportu-*
> *nity and promise*
> *for all who seek to*
> *advance*
> *and achieve.*
>
> —Ileana Ros-Lehtinen

In 1989, the longtime U.S. representative in Ros-Lehtinen's district, Claude Pepper, died. Encouraged by the national Republican leadership, Ros-Lehtinen resigned her state senate seat and ran in the special election to succeed him. The district, Florida's 18th, is heavily Cuban American but also has African-American and Jewish neighborhoods. Many senior citizens live throughout the area.

After winning a four-way race for the Republican nomination, she defeated her Democratic opponent, Gerald Richman, in the general election with 53 percent of the vote. The various ethnic groups voted very differently. Cuban Americans, who represented 37 percent of registered voters, turned out in large numbers and gave her 90 percent of their votes. It was enough to overcome her much lower voting percentages from other groups, which historically voted for Democrats. She has since been reelected in 1990, 1992, 1994, and 1996 by large margins, sometimes running unopposed.

During her career in the U.S. House of Representatives, Ros-Lehtinen has generally been considered a conservative Republican, though she is more independent in voting on educational issues. Through the years, she has concentrated her efforts on behalf of freedom and liberty within Cuba. She is an unrelenting opponent of Fidel Castro's Marxist ideology, reflecting the opinion of many Cubans and Cuban Americans in her Miami district.

Ros-Lehtinen's policy to achieve a democratic Cuba has three main points. First, the U.S. should maintain or strengthen its trade and other restrictions on Cuba's economy until Castro is forced to change his policies. Second, Castro must leave office or at least hold free elections. Third, anyone who goes to Cuba to see Castro should also visit Castro's political opponents and call for free elections.

She often differs with official U.S. policy that takes a harder line against other dictatorships than it does against Cuba. One example of her differing in opinion occurred after a 1996 investigation into drug-smuggling in south Florida that may have had a connection to the Cuba government. In a speech on the House floor, Ros-Lehtinen said that the war on drugs will fail unless the government addresses Castro's role in smuggling. "It is time to expose the tyrant's involvement and lift the veil of silence on his complicity in drug smuggling." She asked when were U.S. antidrug agencies going to stop dragging their heels and look for proof of Castro's involvement.

She also related this governmental silence to other nations. She says that allies who stood with the United States against undemocratic regimes in Haiti, South Africa, Iraq, and elsewhere have ignored Cuba, "preferring to gain a quick and easy dollar from the repression against the people on the island." Still, she voices her faith that the United States and other nations will "make that dream of freedom a reality for the enslaved people of Cuba."

She has been a chief spokesperson for a tougher U.S. policy against Cuba and against Castro. U.S. trade with Cuba was banned in the early 1960s. Several other restrictive trade laws were passed after that. The United States took a further step in 1995 with passage of the Cuban Liberty and Democratic Solidarity Act—usually called the "Helms-Burton" Act—which penalizes other countries that operate in Cuba.

In 1995, several representatives wanted to lead a trade delegation to Cuba. Ros-Lehtinen objected, saying that such a mission would loosen the trade embargo. She protested to President Bill Clinton that it was important to make it clear that the United States will "penalize anyone who willingly violates the embargo."

In the past, the Cuban government seized American property and then allowed friendlier governments and foreign companies to invest in it. Helms-Burton lets the government forbid entry of such investors into the United States, meaning they can't invest or trade here. The European Union filed an objection against Helms-Burton with the World Trade Organization (WTO), saying it was a law that extended beyond the boundaries of the United States.

Ros-Lehtinen chairs two subcommittees—Africa and the Western Hemisphere—in the Committee on International Relations. She was part of a congressional delegation that, in 1996, went to various European capitals to explain Helms-Burton. She spoke out frequently to explain the U.S. position. However, in 1998, the European Union dropped its case.

Ros-Lehtinen also spoke out about the "Brothers to the Rescue" incident. In 1996, a Miami-based anti-Castro humanitarian group, Brothers to the Rescue, patroled the nearby ocean in small, unarmed planes, dropping supplies to Cuban refugees trying to reach the United States, often on homemade, leaky rafts.

In February 1996, two of the group's planes were shot down by Cuban military aircraft. Four fliers died, three of them U.S. citizens. Cuba's excuse was that the planes were in Cuban air space. President Clinton and then-ambassador to the United Nations Madeleine Albright condemned the Cuban action.

Ros-Lehtinen went further. Calling Castro a "beast" and a "tyrant," she asked for the same kind of U.S. naval blockade against Cuba that was used against Haiti (another Caribbean nation) several years earlier. A year later, she explained how the Brothers to the Rescue deaths were just four of the hundreds of people killed by the Castro government as they tried to leave Cuba. It was in the name of these people, she said, that Helms-Burton had been passed.

Late in 1997, a U.S. court awarded $187 million to the families of the three U.S. citizens killed in the incident. It was the first case tried under the federal Anti-Terrorism and Effective Death Penalty Act of 1996. The money would have to be collected from the Cuban Air Force. This is unlikely; however, some of the funds could be collected from Cuban assets held by the U.S. government.

Ros-Lehtinen has also taken independent stands in relation to the Republican party and to the Congressional Hispanic Caucus. She broke with Republican leadership over a proposal to make English the official language of the United States. English is our main language, but it has never been legally designated as the official language. Many immigrant groups, including the Congressional Hispanic Caucus, have opposed such a law because they believe it would destroy their heritage.

Ros-Lehtinen in 1996, showing the picture of a mentally disabled immigrant whose public assistance payments may be cut off under the new welfare law (AP/Wide World Photos)

ILEANA ROS-LEHTINEN

The proposal to make English the official language (called the English Language Empowerment Act of 1996) was proposed by the House Republican leadership, which included Speaker Newt Gingrich. But in a floor speech, Ros-Lehtinen objected as a public servant, an educator, and a mother. By being a multilingual nation, with English as the primary but not official language, the United States would continue to reinforce the acceptance of diversity, she said. The United States would continue to be a nation where "differences, not similarities are the norm. . . ." The nation's heritage, she said, "is not so much English itself," but that "we have been given the honor of all being Americans."

The fact that all Americans benefit from the nation's democratic ideals and liberties "is a far more cohesive bond than any language could ever be," she said. Finally, for school students who are not yet comfortable with English, English-only education would "prove to be a disservice."

The bill passed in the House, but was not acted on by the Senate. By siding on this issue with the largely Democratic Hispanic Caucus, she gained more influence within the caucus.

Early in 1997, however, she split with the caucus on another issue. The new chairman of the caucus, Xavier Becerra (a Democrat from California), had recently met with Fidel Castro in Cuba. Believing that the 1960s boycott actually harms the Cuban people, he sought a closer relationship with Castro. But, he failed to call for free elections or to visit with Castro's political opponents—two requirements in Ros-Lehtinen's position on Cuba. She resigned from the caucus in protest.

Always a supporter of the Cuban-American community's needs, Ros-Lehtinen was one of only two Republican House members who voted against the 1996 welfare reform bill. This was because it removed legal immigrants' ability to seek welfare benefits. (This was restored in 1998.) She asked the Immigration and Naturalization Service to bypass some requirements for citizenship so that disabled legal immigrants can become Americans.

Ros-Lehtinen is intensely proud of her Cuban origins, and encourages her own children to be bilingual. She often says to them, "español," reminding them to speak Spanish, so that the heritage will continue with the next generation.

Chronology

Further Reading

Congressional Record, February 27, 1996, p. H1256. Ros-Lehtinen's remarks about Cuba's shooting down of planes belonging to members of Brothers to the Rescue.

Congressional Record, August 1, 1996, p. H9725. Ros-Lehtinen's remarks about the proposed English Language Empowerment Act of 1996.

"Drive to Stiffen Cuba Embargo Fails." *1995 CQ Almanac,* pp. 10–21. Background, including Ros-Lehtinen's position, in a bill to tighten the embargo on Cuba.

Hoffman, David. "Bush Boosts Candidate for Pepper's House Seat." *Washington Post,* August 17, 1989, p. A4. Discussion of Ros-Lehtinen's first campaign for a seat in the House of Representatives.

Hohler, Bob. "Moakley's Cuba Trade Visit Plan Hit by Anti-Castro Lawmakers.' *Boston Globe,* August 28, 1997, Reprinted on http://www.latinolink.com/biz/cuba1102.html. Discussion of Ros-Lehtinen's (and others) position on American Congressmembers' proposed visit to Cuba.

Meier, Matt S. "Ileana Ros-Lehtinen." *Notable Latino Americans.* Westport, Conn.: Greenwood Press, 1997. Biographical profile of Ros-Lehtinen.

Navarro, Mireya. "U.S. Judge Assesses Cuba in Pilot Killings." *New York Times,* December 18, 1997, p. A20. Discusses the U.S. court decision to assess damages against the Cuban Air Force for the killings of members of Brothers to the Rescue.

Parker, Laura. "Cuban Americans Lead in Races for House Seat." *Washington Post,* July 30, 1989, p. A3. Discussion of campaign of Ros-Lehtinen and others to win a seat in the House.

Schmalz, Jeffrey. "Cuban Emigre Wins Election to U.S. House." *New York Times,* August 31, 1989, p. A16. Discussion of Ros-Lehtinen's victory in her first House campaign.

Biographical material is available at the following website:

http://www.vote-smart.org

Index

Italic numbers indicate illustrations. **Boldface** numbers indicate main topics. Page numbers followed by *c* indicate chronology.